ARCADE MANIA!

ARCADE MANIA!

ARCADE MANIA!

THE TURBO-CHARGED WORLD OF JAPAN'S GAME CENTERS

BRIAN ASHCRAFT

WITH JEAN SNOW

FOREWORDS BY KEVIN WILLIAMS
AND BRIAN CRECENTE

KODANSHA INTERNATIONAL
TOKYO · NEW YORK · LONDON

Distributed in the United States by Kodansha America, LLC,
and in the United Kingdom and Continental Europe by Kodansha Europe Ltd.

Published by Kodansha International Ltd., 17-14 Otowa 1-chome,
Bunkyo-ku, Tokyo 112-8652.

First edition, 2008
17 16 15 14 13 12 11 10 09 08   10 9 8 7 6 5 4 3 2 1

Library of Congress Cataloging-in-Publication Data

Ashcraft, Brian.
Arcade mania : the turbo-charged world of Japan's game centers /
Brian Ashcraft with Jean Snow.
       p. cm.
  Includes index.
  ISBN 978-4-7700-3078-8
  1. Pinball machines--Japan. 2. Arcades--Japan. 3. Games--
Japan. I. Snow, Jean. II. Title.
  GV1311.P5A74 2008
  794.7'50952--dc22
                                       2008023389

www.kodansha-intl.com

ARCADE MANIA! CONTENTS

ゲーセン
マニア

A WORD FROM *THE INDUSTRY . . .*

So you've picked up this book, thumbed through the pages—and now you're hooked! I'm honored to be invited by the authors to write a foreword for this impressively crafted compendium of the marvels of the Japanese amusement-arcade scene. Whether you're feeling nostalgic for past arcade glories, or relishing the chance to read about the thrills and spills of the world of Japanese arcade games, this book is a fascinating insight into the development of the country's amusement industry, focusing on the people that are part of it.

KEVIN WILLIAMS

For many, the recent success of the current-generation home-console scene has sidetracked any interest in video amusement, with many commentators feeling that the arcade industry is dead—a point of view based on ignorance of the market and aggravated by the sometimes poor communication between the Western and Asian amusement industries. But coin-op still fires players' imaginations, as shown recently by long lines of eager players waiting to get their hands on the latest arcade installment of the *Street Fighter* series, and a host of new developments—many of which you'll find detailed in this book—proving that the arcade-game genre is alive and well.

The arcade scene in Japan offers a dazzling and compelling environment for players and audience, and as with the Japanese love affair with technology, the new trends that stir the Asian buying public today will soon be reflected in the American and European markets.

I was asked to write this foreword by the authors because of my unique position in what I call the "out-of-home interactive entertainment" industry. I have been on both sides of the table as regards working in the amusement and attraction scene, both developing and selling the technology; bitten by the arcade bug back in the 1970s with my first game of Atari's *Lunar Lander*. Once a Walt

Disney Imagineer, I am now head of KWP Limited, one of the few consultancies that specializes in the amusement and attraction industry sector; a prolific provider of written reports on the amusement scene for trade and consumer journals and publisher of the specialist international industry e-newsletter *The Stinger Report*, read by many in the amusement and attraction trade, and by the players themselves.

Coming from this background, it is great to see *Arcade Mania!* present the "turbo-charged" landscape of Japanese amusement in such a colourful manner to a brand new audience—enjoy.

KEVIN WILLIAMS
AMUSEMENT INDUSTRY CONSULTANT AND WRITER

||||||||
A WORD FROM *A GAMER* . . .

Growing up in the seventies, an army brat of sorts, arcade games kept me company as my family ping-ponged across oceans and countries. It didn't matter where we moved, everywhere from Thailand to Texas had arcades, making each new home feel welcoming. Reading through this book taps into those memories: days spent in an empty arcade in Korea playing shoot 'em ups; hours spent in an Officer's Club playing *Frogger*; my first *Street Fighter* fireball at a Texas bowling alley.

It wasn't until I was managing an arcade in college, years later, that I realized that the arcade cacophony, the flashing lights, the pocket full of quarters, were the hallmarks of a whole generation's childhood memories. In Japan, those memories are still being formed in places like Akihabara, the arcade-laden town of Shangri-La-like import for North American gamers, but the arcades of the West have long since fallen.

But don't mourn the fall of America's arcades, a place of pinball, not pachinko; of ticket games, not card games. Instead celebrate the confluence of culture and technology still thriving in Japan.

BRIAN CRECENTE
MANAGING EDITOR
OF KOTAKU.COM,
GAMER

BRIAN CRECENTE

STEP INSIDE. PASSING ROWS OF CRANE GAMES, THE AIR IS THICK WITH GRAY CIGARETTE SMOKE AS *PLAYERS FEED COINS INTO SLOTS.*

Arcade staff empty ashtrays and wipe down cabinets between rounds of play. Groups of schoolgirls pile into sticker-picture booths. Mild-mannered salarymen display impressive *King of Fighters* fighting skills. A few of the game cabinets are connected to flat-screen TVs so bystanders can stop and ogle. Grimy VCRs are hooked up to bullet-hell shooting games, making it possible for players to record their game play, take home the VHS tape, and study. A line has formed for card-based game *Sangokushi Taisen*, snaking past the latest dizzying *beatmania* rhythm game from Konami. Housewives carry buckets of worthless tokens for roaring pachinko machines. A blue plastic gun is pulled and fired at a monitor. *Bang bang!* The Sega rally-car pedal is pushed to the metal. And players just keep playing. Welcome to the game center, the Japanese arcade. This is where regular folks show off irregular game skills.

Arcades in the US are dead. Arcades in Japan? Evolving. From their humble, analog beginnings atop department stores in the 1960s to their *Space Invader* explosion in coffee houses during the 1970s, Japanese arcades are always reinventing themselves, trying to create something that can only be experienced in the arcade environment. Gaming fads have come and gone, but game centers remain. They're not gonna go away quietly! That, right there, is exactly why they matter. Facing competition from home consoles like never before, Japanese arcades and arcade players keep on keepin' on, knowing that the game-center experience can never be replicated in the home.

There's a lot of history in *Arcade Mania!*, but that doesn't mean that it's a history book. This book doesn't even attempt to catalog every single Japanese arcade game, because your neighborhood game center doesn't have every single game. *Arcade Mania!* is your tour guide, offering a window into arcades: the games, the people who make them, and the players. Chapter by chapter, the book is broken down like the sections of an arcade. It starts with crane games and moves on to sticker-picture >>>>>>>

booths, because that's what you typically see when walking into a game center off the street. Venturing further into this amalgamized arcade, there are rhythm games, shooting games, fighting games, games of chance, dedicated cabinets, retro games, and card-based games. This book brings the Japanese arcade experience to you the reader wherever you are—all that's missing is the squeak of linoleum under your sneakers, the stench of stale cigarette smoke, and the plane ticket to Tokyo.

An arcade is only as good as its games, as its players. And we've talked to the players who inhabit these arcades. Why, in an age where home consoles dominate, do they still make the trip to game centers? These are not casual players, they are hard-core players—"maniacs," as the Japanese would call them. From a housewife who features in instructional videos for crane games to a Hitachi R&D researcher who loves arcade shooting games so much that he programs his own, they're individuals who have devoted themselves to their chosen game.

While I was writing this book, I'd bicycle to my neighborhood arcade for a quick fifteen- or thirty-minute play session. Compared to the hours and hours necessary to finish a home-console game, a quick game or two would satisfy that gaming urge. Besides, it was "research"! This wasn't my first taste of the arcade scene—I cover games and Japan for popular gaming blog Kotaku.com where I'm an editor, and *Wired* magazine, where I'm a contributing editor. My work on Japan and technology has also appeared in *Popular Science*, *Metropolis* magazine, and *The Japan Times*. Covering Japan is a great beat. Covering games in Japan is even better.

"Home console games are like novels," says top Sega game designer Yu Suzuki, "arcade games are like poems." There's a great deal of passion, purity, and spent coins in these game centers. Poetry, too.

BRIAN ASHCRAFT
OSAKA, 2008

START

A MOUNTAIN OF CUDDLY TOY BEARS LIES BENEATH A HANGING MECHANICAL CLAW.

Faces pressed against the glass of the cabinet, the bears at the bottom are distorted by the weight of those above. They seem a little sad, distressed even—as if they need rescuing. Luckily help is on the way.

Dressed in a black two-piece ensemble with black knee-high boots—attractively yet modestly accessorized with a silver bracelet and a Patrick Cox hand-bag—Yuka Nakajima doesn't look like most people's idea of a gamer. She could easily be mistaken for a woman out on the town for a bit of shopping, or maybe on her way to meet girlfriends at a café. But Nakajima is on a mission.

THE CATCHER QUEEN SURVEYS HER REALM

Maneuvering her way through the maze of pachinko parlors, host clubs, and hostess bars in the red-light district west of Tokyo's Ikebukuro Station, Nakajima arrives at the Rosa Building, home of the Taito Station game center. Without hesitation, she makes her way through the bright red entrance bearing Taito's

YUKA NAKAJIMA IS THE UFO CATCHER QUEEN

THE ROSA BUILDING IN IKEBUKURO   YUKA NAKAJIMA

trademark *Space Invader* logo. This place is clearly well known to her, and, once inside, she quickly starts her rounds, pausing in front of various glass cases then moving on. Eventually she comes to a halt in front of a glass cabinet full of toy bears. Her head tilts slightly to the side as she sizes up the scene before her. Yuka Nakajima is the UFO Catcher Queen, and she is here to catch her prize.

"UFO Catcher" is the most popular term for the various incarnations of crane or claw games that are usually found at the entrance of Japanese game centers. These bright, colorful machines, brimming with attractive, eye-catching, and seemingly easily attainable prizes, are there to lure people who normally wouldn't venture inside a game center. Add a reasonable price to the equation (just one hundred yen for one play, or five hundred yen for six) and many are tempted to have a go on one of the vast array of crane games that stand sentry at the doors of the nation's arcades.

Most of the machines are produced by one of the big three crane-game makers: Sega, Taito, and Namco Bandai Games Inc. (NBGI). A particular type of play characterizes each company's machines. Basically, however, the idea is always the same—manipulate a claw, grab one of the prizes in the glass case, and drop it through a hole where it can be claimed by the player. Simple! But these games are harder than they look. And as players try and try again to win a prize, the coins they feed into the slots contribute generously to the game center's bottom line. It's big business: the Japan Amusement Machinery Manufacturers' Association (JAMMA) reported a crane- and prize-game revenue of 250 billion yen in 2005, a figure that represented a whopping 40 percent of all game revenues at arcades in Japan for that year.

FROM TOP: THE *ERIE DIGGER*, SEGA'S *GROUP SKILL DIGA* AND *DIGA MART* (NOTE THE UFO)

Of the three grand poobahs, Japanese arcade industry leader Sega was one of the pioneers of Japan's crane-game business with its *Skill Diga* in 1965, inspired by what is believed to be the first of such games, *The Erie Digger*, which first appeared in the US in the late nineteenth century. *Skill Diga* was later joined by other "diggers," *Super Skill Diga* (1968), *Diga Mart* (1983), and *New Skill Diga* (1984). Then in 1985, Sega came up with the *UFO Catcher*, a game so successful that the name is now synonymous with the crane-game genre. Interestingly, it was called the *Eagle Catcher* during development,

until it was pointed out that the shape of the claw resembled a UFO.

All sorts of *UFO Catchers* followed: *DXes, Minis, Exes*; a slim space-saving version called *Baby UFO*; the 360-degree view *Dream Palace* series; the *MAXEdition*, with larger prizes, brighter cases, and extra cushioning to soften the impact as the large prizes fell; and also the enticingly named *UFO Colon*, with an alternative display method using trays, and with easier functionality, to encourage children to play. The basic *UFO Catcher* series, however, is still going strong, in its eighth iteration at the time of writing.

While Sega was catching spacecraft, NBGI debuted with sweets in 1986. The *SweetLand* series used a scoop instead of claw, and it wasn't until 2001 that it introduced a crane game, the *WideWideClipper*. With its lengthy claw, and adjustable grips moving from either ends of a larger rectangular base, the

©NBGI

ABOVE: *UFO CATCHER 8* AND *CLENAWIDE* PICKED CLEAN. BELOW: *SWEETLAND4 BRIGHT*

Clipper was perfect for larger or boxed prizes. The *WideWideClipper Blue Version* was released in 2002 (the new "fresh" color change made to target adults), and in 2004 came the *ClenaFlex*, which has a more traditional claw mechanism and is one of NBGI's most popular machines. The *ClenaWide*, launched in 2006, saw the return of the *WideWide*-style claw. NBGI's scoop machines have remained popular over the years and the *SweetLand4* and *SweetLandPremia* machines can still be found in most game centers.

©NBGI

PLAYER 1

NAME: YUKA NAKAJIMA
SPECIALTY: CRANE GAMES
**FAVORITE GAME: CRANE GAMES
WITH RILAKKUMA**

TOP 5 TIPS:

1. FIND THE RIGHT MACHINE.

Finding the right machine is part of the art of great crane catching. "The staff can control how strong or weak the claw is," explains catcher queen Yuka Nakajima. "After one try, you can immediately tell when the claw setting is too weak." Staff at game centers adjust the strength of the claw in the "interest" of making it fair for everyone, and they are also instructed on how prizes are to be laid out inside the case. If you spend enough time in a game center, you'll start noticing staff testing the machine after they have placed the prizes inside the case, to make sure that it isn't too easy to be a winner.

2. PRACTICE MAKES PERFECT.

It's only through constant practice that you'll become skilled in moving the claw. The expert crane-game player has developed a feel for the way the claw moves, how fast it should move, and what kind of force you need to get from point A to point B. Timing is critical.

3. LOOK FOR THE HOOK.

Be on the lookout for anything that sticks out from the mountain of prizes piled up inside the cabinet. If there's a tag, try to grab it, if it's a plush doll, go for folded arms, or if the prize is boxed, go for the lid. The goal is to go for anything that has a part that the claw can hook into.

4. THE HOLE IS THE GOAL.

Go for prizes that are located near the hole, so that a lunge of the claw can topple them over.

5. THE EARLY BIRD CATCHES THE WORM.

Get to the game center as soon as it opens, usually at ten in the morning, which is when you'll find the best placements for prizes, unspoiled by amateur tries that may have created impossible arrangements.

Taito's presence is strong, mostly due to the abundance of Taito game centers. Taito's crane games bear the brand name *Capriccio*, and they include the *Capriccio Sesame 2ᵅ* (2006) which has brought to the scene a claw that promises a wider angle and better grips.

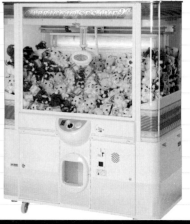

© TAITO CORP. 2006 POSTPET TM
© SO-NET ENTERTAINMENT CORPORATION

TAITO'S *CAPRICCIO SESAME 2ᵅ*

Back in Ikebukuro, at the Taito Station game center, Yuka Nakajima is hard at work. "Each machine has different advantages," she says. "Taito's joystick mechanism gives you more control. You can make small, precise movements, and you're allowed a lot of tries within the time limit. With Sega, it's more about moving the crane to the left and right, and then front and back, but one of the plus points is that you can sometimes stop the arm." With NBGI, it's another aspect of the design that gets a twist. Nakajima explains: "There's usually more than one hole to drop the prize in, and you can control the extent to which the claw opens."

In her late thirties, and mother of two young children, Nakajima was not always such an expert on these games. In fact her induction into the world of crane games was relatively recent. Unlike those with memories of playing as a child, nostalgia pushing them to play years later, Nakajima was instead driven by a desire to help a certain creature in need—the cuddly Rilakkuma bear.

"It was 2003 when these bears first started to appear as crane-game prizes," recalls Nakajima. "And when I saw them, I just had to rescue them," she laughs. So far, her humanitarian effort to free as many of the bears as possible has seen her bring freedom to over 3,500 of them (and counting). She gives away most of her winnings to friends and family, but the Rilakkuma (the name combines the Japanese pronunciation of "relax" and *kuma*, the Japanese word for "bear") remains her target and obsession. An entire room of her apartment has become a Rilakkuma sanctuary. "I never buy them though," she insists. "I only rescue them from game centers."

Nakajima's obsession led to the development of her incredible crane-game skills. Her quick assessment of the way prizes are arranged in a particular crane-game cabinet, her instinctive feel for whether success is attainable, and her effortlessly fast handling of the controls immediately reveal a level of confidence that you don't see with casual players. While she never actively tried to become the "queen" of the crane-game scene, there was a point when she realized she had attained a level of expertise that was beyond the norm. "It was when I went to Ikebukuro by bicycle and then had to go home by taxi because I had won too many Rilakkuma bears," says Nakajima. "That felt good."

Stuffed toys, including the ever-popular Walt Disney family of character goods, are the staple of the crane-game case, but from >>>>>>>>

"I HAD TO GO HOME BY TAXI BECAUSE I HAD WON TOO MANY RILAKKUMA BEARS"

RILAKKUMA BEARS WAITING TO BE RESCUED

CRANE GAMES LURE IN THE PUNTERS

THE QUEEN'S SPEECH

Just how good a crane-game player is the UFO Catcher Queen? So good, in fact, that Sega enlisted the aid of Yuka Nakajima in the production of video lessons that are shown at some game centers. The videos, played on a monitor encased in glass and surrounded by prizes, are there to give players a few tips on how to improve their chances of winning a prize. Following a brief setup in which various players, such as a pair of giggling schoolgirls, or an office worker and his upset wife, appear to have no luck in their play sessions, it's the UFO Catcher Queen to the rescue! Appearing in

a floating bubble in a corner of the screen, she hands out advice in the form of lessons that illustrate all of the strategies she uses herself when playing.

there, prizes enter new realms of extravagance. What's for dinner? How about those packs of military rations—maybe kimchi pilaf or paella—you won earlier in the day? And girls will love getting samples of the latest perfumes. Snacks (from chocolate to chips) are of course covered, both individual packs and huge, family-sized boxes, as are the latest action figures (with *Gundam* always a favorite). Some prizes are even useful. "I've gotten a rice cooker, as well as an ice-cream maker," says Nakajima. "I use both."

Nakajima's wizardry has led to frequent TV appearances, as well as invitations to various game-related competitions. At the All Nippon Amusement Machine Operators' Union expo in February 2008 she emceed the National Crane-Game Championships. She's also the star of an instructional video explaining how to succeed at crane games that can be seen in game centers up and down the land. But soon even the UFO Catcher Queen may have to update her skills: crane games are changing and recently a new dimension has been added to the basic lunge-and-claw concept.

It was perhaps inevitable that in robot-crazy Japan, crane games too would undergo a robotic evolution. *Robo Catcher* by Fukuoka-based MechaTraX may just be the start. "Our company started with the research and development of a small two-legged robot in the summer of 2004," explains MechaTraX CEO Soichi Nagasato. "It had nothing to do with the amusement industry; our main customers were universities and research laboratories. But it was a highly specialized and not very profitable market—we would only manufacture about ten models a year. So in the spring of 2006, we started considering new, more profitable business models." The company carried out research into various industries that might benefit from the robot technology it had already invested in. It soon became apparent that

ROBO CATCHER IN ACTION

the amusement market was an ideal target. "From a marketing standpoint, we came to realize that an arcade-game machine using a humanoid robot would be a surefire winner," says Nagasato. "With more than 120 thousand crane-game machines operating in Japan, and sales of the equipment reaching 200 billion yen a year, it's the category with the highest sales." Armed with this knowledge, it didn't take MechaTraX long to come up with *Robo Catcher*, a charming variation on the ubiquitous crane game.

In *Robo Catcher*, you quite literally take control of a two-legged robot, moving him around his "cell" by using four directional buttons. Two other buttons are used to try to grab a prize and then dump it into the dispenser slot. Playing will run you a hundred or two hundred yen, with a time limit between thirty and sixty seconds (the price and time limit are at the discretion of the game center) giving you as many tries as the countdown will allow. If the robot falls over, the touch of a button will have him scrambling to his feet, using his arms to steady himself.

So far *Robo Catcher* has been a huge hit with players—getting geeks and techno nerds who normally wouldn't set foot near a crane game to finally give the prize machines a try—and also with the gaming industry. At Japan's 45th Amusement Machine Show in >>>>>

MECHATRAX CEO SOICHI NAGASATO

THE NATIONAL CRANE-GAME CHAMPIONSHIPS

Take it from the UFO Catcher Queen, Yuka Nakajima, crane gaming is not all about luck. It's a game of skill. In 2006, to highlight the talents of Japan's top crane gamers and elect one supreme crane-game master, the National Crane-Game Championships was inaugurated. Since then it's been a regular event at Tokyo's annual Amusement Machine Operators' Union Expo. The 2008 tourney saw reigning champ (and two-time winner) Nakajima switch her competitor status to that of commentator, giving the proceedings the air of authority that only a pro athlete can bring to the sport they represent.

The stage was set with eight crane-game cabinets—four of Sega's *UFO Catcher 8* machines and four of Taito's *Capriccio Cone HG*— and twenty-two regional champions, all vying to become the one true master of the crane. Competitors were a varied bunch, from a six-year-old girl who impressed the crowd with the skills of a seasoned veteran, to a housewife wearing an apron. As a surprise bonus to all, it was announced that the winner would face off against Nakajima.

For the first round of play, participants were divided into

three groups: two groups of eight, and one group of six. Each player had five tries at each of the eight cabinets, where they had to contend with prizes of all shapes and sizes: giant *Sesame Street* character heads; Rilakkuma bears; tiny Marimokkori mascot dolls, whose round green shape is based on a type of algae ball found in lakes in

A YOUNG COMPETITOR TAKES CONTROL

Japan's northernmost prefecture of Hokkaido; and boxed dolls of popular characters Tensai Bakabon or Kamen Rider—the latter the trickiest according to commentator Nakajima, who confessed to the audience that capturing boxes is her biggest weakness.

The mesmerized audience watched with bated breath as the winner of the most prizes in each group emerged—with nineteen, ⌄⌄

twenty, and twenty-one prizes respectively—to secure a place in the final three. Following a half-time show featuring a five-girl team of dancers decked out in cowboy hats, angel wings, and furry tiger-print hot pants complete with tail, it was on to the nerve-racking final. Here, the three finalists had fifteen minutes to capture as many prizes as they could, an unexpectedly exciting spectacle as they

In the end, it was a tie between Aya Toyoda and Yosuke Ishii, who had to battle it out in sudden death style: a succession of rounds in which each player has one turn on the machine of their choice, and the first player unable to match the other's catch loses. In the opening round, Ishii went first and missed, but Toyoda picked up a boxed Tensai Bakabon, sweeping to victory on her first try. The

THE QUEEN VS. AYA TOYODA

THE COMPETITORS

frantically ran from one available cabinet to the next, quickly positioning the crane and then darting off to the next machine, not even waiting to see if they had captured anything (the judges took good care of that).

sixteen-year-old proved that her win was no fluke when her face-off with the UFO Catcher Queen turned into a blowout. The winner of this final challenge would be the first player to capture two Marimokkori dolls. Reigning queen Nakajima was empty-clawed on her first attempt, but in less than ten seconds Toyoda had grabbed two dolls at once!

Long live the new queen!

2007, *Robo Catcher* made an impressive showing, reaching the top three in the Most Popular Game Machine category. "The top ten is usually entirely made up of international game machine manufacturers, such as Sega and NBGI, so for a small firm like ours to achieve such a high ranking is something I'm very proud of," explains Nagasato, who believes that an emotional response to the robot may be the reason for its success. "Using a humanoid two-legged robot, the feeling is quite different from other types of crane games. Play is more instinctual, and you start empathizing with the robotic avatar in a big way." Much like Nakajima is driven by empathy to rescue Rilakkuma, perhaps.

Following a morning session that has taken Nakajima through several of Ikebukuro's many game centers, she exits the Sunshine Street branch of the Adores chain—her favorite, and one of the most prominent arcades in the area—with no winnings in hand. Even the UFO Catcher Queen cannot exert complete control over the cranes and robots that populate her stuffed-animal kingdom. "Some days I know I won't catch anything," admits Nakajima, visibly regretting that she didn't live up to her esteemed status of crane-game royalty. "But I will never stop playing," vows the queen, with a determined toss of her stylishly coiffed head. She slings her Patrick Cox bag over her shoulder, and disappears into the crowd, leaving the bears to another day of captivity. ✵

ROBO FIGHTERS

What's next for MechaTrax? If a robot-based crane machine is not the first thing that comes to mind when imagining where amusement and robots might meet, the thought of robots fighting it out in a ring is surely something many gamers have dreamed of seeing. MechaTraX is on the case. "We would love to develop a robot-game machine of the fighting or grappling type," says CEO Nagasato, "although this may not happen for a few years yet."

CUTE NEVER DIES. IT ONLY FADES.

And even then. If you're young and female, the Japanese term for cute, *kawaii*, isn't just a word. Oh no. From glossy pink cell phones to glossy pink gals, kawaii is a lifestyle. Inside this sticker-picture booth, a liquid-crystal display shows in real time what the digital camera above sees: twenty-five-year-old model Rina Sakurai—better known to her fans as Sakurina—wearing impossibly short shorts and sporting fingernails ornately decorated with miniature plastic donuts and ice-cream cones. "Sticker pictures make you look better than real life," she says. In the sticker-picture booth,

KAWAII IS MORE THAN JUST A WORD

:いコースをタッチしてね

Rich
Madonna
華やかでキレイ
リッチマドンナ

Paradise
Girl
ポップ　キュート
パラ　　　ール

MAKING YOU LOOK BETTER THAN REAL LIFE

bright white lights encased in plastic surround the camera. Sakurina ruffles her nest of dyed blond hair, and the lights change to a
soft yellow and then to a gentle blue. "Ooooooh, wow!" she gushes,
just before she pouts her lips and poses, as the snap of the shutter
sounds through the booth. Welcome to Fantasyland.

"I've easily taken several thousand sticker pictures," says Sakurina. "I've lost count." For Sakurina, taking sticker pictures is more
than a simple hobby, it's a calling. She's sitting on the twelfth floor
of Make Software, maker of sticker-picture machines, holding curl-
ing irons to her hair and flipping through a magazine that features
her on the cover. An exclusive model for cutesy fashion magazine
Koakuma Ageha, Sakurina started out as one of those candy-coated
models that appear on the outside of sticker-picture booths. When
she was sixteen years old, Sakurina was discovered in a south
Osaka arcade by a Make Software scout while taking sticker pics
with her buddies. After coming in first place in a Make Software-
sponsored amateur-model sticker-picture contest, she found herself
a working model. "I didn't know which machine I was going to be
on," Sakurina recalls, examining the donuts and ice-cream cones

FOR SAKURINA, STICKER PICS ARE A CALLING

"I'VE EASILY TAKEN SEVERAL THOUSAND STICKER PICTURES," SAYS SAKURINA. "I'VE LOST COUNT."

on her fingernails. She and some pals were in some random arcade when they stumbled upon Sakurina's smiling face plastered all over a Make Software booth. "It was kind of funny," she says. "We took snapshots of me standing in front of the machine."

Photo booths are a regular part of the Japanese urban landscape and have been since the postwar era. But the sticker-picture machine is the photo booth redux. Here's how it works: the booth houses a digital printer, a PC, a digital camera, and an in-booth LCD display so that sitters can see what pics are being taken. Users pose in front of a green screen and can choose from an endless selection of CG backgrounds, ranging from schoolyards to the Sahara Desert. Multiple pics are snapped by the camera (some machines even have two—one for close-ups, one for full-body photographs) and teens can pick their favorite ones using the touchscreen. After posing for >>>>>>>>

WHEN KIDS GO OUT THEY TYPICALLY END UP PILING INTO A STICKER-PICTURE BOOTH TO COMMEMORATE THE EVENT

A REGULAR PART OF JAPANESE YOUTH CULTURE

photos, gals then scribble digital notes, called *rakugaki* in Japanese, and can add a variety of other decorations via a touchscreen located outside the booth. Less than a minute later, a sheet of anywhere between sixteen and twenty pics is printed out. Since game centers typically provide scissors for sticker-picture-cuttin', gals divvy up the pictures among themselves. Taking sticker pictures, Sakurina points out, has become a regular part of Japanese youth culture. When kids go out, they typically end up piling into a sticker-picture booth to commemorate the event.

Thanks to the economic bubble and a largely middle-class society, Japanese teens in the early 1990s had endless disposable pocket money. For teenage dudes, that meant hitting the local arcades to spend the equivalent of thirty or forty bucks on *Street Fighter II*. For teenage gals, that meant either shopping with gal pals at Tokyo shopping haven Shibuya 109 or being dragged around smoke-filled game centers on "dates." All that changed in 1995.

PLAYER 2

NAME: SAKURINA
SPECIALTY: STICKER PICTURES
FAVORITE MACHINE: BIJIN NI NARIMASHO ("BE A BEAUTIFUL GIRL")

First time in a sticker-pic booth? Sakurina's here to help. Besides being a professional sticker-picture model, she's the exclusive face of Japanese fashion magazine *Koakuma Ageha*. The big difference between doing fashion shoots and sticker pictures? "There're fewer people standing around when you do sticker pics," says Sakurina. "That, and you can check what the camera's seeing via the in-booth monitor." So, let's have it—Sakurina's advice for the perfect sticker-pic:

TOP 5 TIPS:

1. PRACTICE MAKES PERFECT.
Take lots and lots of photos of yourself in advance and figure out your best angle.

2. TO SMILE OR NOT TO SMILE?
If you have a chubby face, don't smile because that will make you look chubbier. The opposite is also true: if you have a thin face, say *cheezu!* and smile.

3. LARGE FACE?
While posing for the picture, lower your chin to make your face look smaller.

4. THE EYES HAVE IT.
Open your eyes wide for doe-eyed anime cuteness.

5. BE SPONTANEOUS!
While doing rakugaki, don't think too much! Just select the digital designs and write whatever you want.

Forever. A year earlier, the then twenty-nine-year-old Miho Sasaki, employee at Japanese arcade-game developer Atlus, saw that home-video editing machines were able to superimpose titles on pictures and then print them out. Sasaki then recalled her own love of cute stickers when she was younger and how she'd put them all over her notebooks. She came up with a new idea that mixed young Japanese females' love of stickers and their love of taking photos of themselves: sticker pictures. Sasaki's idea was initially rejected. Who the hizzy heck wants to take sticker

INSIDE PURIKURA NO MECCA   CHECKING THE RESULTS

pictures of themselves? Not Atlus salarymen in suits, apparently! With fighting games all the rage in the mid-1990s, the idea of a machine that took pictures seemed risky and out of place in arcades packed with game cabinets.

Three months and a new boss after her initial pitch, Sasaki's concept finally found favor with Atlus company president, Naoya Harano. Sega immediately saw potential in the concept and worked with Atlus to codevelop the first sticker-picture machine, called *Print Club*. (*Purikura*, the shortened, Japanized form of the name *Print Club* has become the generic term for the photo stickers.) The digital cameras on the first machines were only able to take lo-res pictures of two or three sitters at the same time, all from the neck up, and with only a few very basic frames as "background." There was no privacy curtain for sitters, and the touchscreen and pens that are now de rigueur weren't yet a feature. *Print Club* unveiled to a lukewarm reception at an industry trade show in February 1995. Sega and Atlus originally tried promoting *Print Club* as something business people could use to take pictures of themselves to put on business cards. The first machines didn't even show up in game centers, but in department store Tokyu Hands. Japan scratched its head, shrugged its shoulders, and was largely indifferent.

Sticker pictures needed more than an industry trade show, business cards, and a department store to get off the ground. They needed a boy band. And not any boy band, but the biggest one in the whole damn country. Yes, sticker pictures needed SMAP, Japan's reigning pop stars, still going strong, and whose members also feature regularly in TV dramas and motion pictures. Hugely popular since 1991, SMAP is a full-blown Japanese institution—like the Post Office, but with better hair. The heartthrobs did sticker pics on their popular television show *SMAPxSMAP*, the phenomenon caught on with high schoolers, and by 1996, sticker pictures

BY 1996, STICKER PICTURES WENT SUPERNOVA AND GALS WERE LINING UP OUTSIDE THE ARCADES FOR THEIR CHANCE TO POSE

went supernova and gals were lining up outside the arcades for their chance to pose. Atlus shipped twenty thousand *Print Club* machines to arcades across Japan. "We believed it would have some success," says Atlus game developer Naoto Hiraoka, responsible for Atlus console games like role-playing game *Shin Megami Tensei* (1992) and doctor simulator *Trauma Center* (2005). "But we never imagined it would be such a huge trend." Calling it "huge" is an understatement and akin to calling a sumo grand champion "husky." *Print Club* was ginormous—so much so that by 1998 the then prime minister Ryutaro Hashimoto installed a Ryu-chan sticker-picture machine in his political party's HQ. The open-to-the-public booth let regular folks take sticker pics with the superimposed smiling politician. In the late 1990s, this was the ultimate photo op!

While Atlus brought the world *Print Club*, Osaka-based company IMS is responsible for the first photo-phonecard booth. Back before cell phones were standard fare, Japan's urban cityscape was dotted with green public payphones that accepted either coins or prepaid phone cards. Around the time Atlus rolled out its first *Print Club* in 1995, IMS released its phone-card picture booth. As with *Print Club*, sitters would pose for pictures, which were then printed on credit-card-sized phone cards instead of stickers. "But when *Print Club* exploded," says IMS president Tomomi Mikage, "it wasn't much of a leap to switch the phone-card

"IT WASN'T MUCH OF A LEAP TO SWITCH THE PHONE-CARD BOOTHS OVER TO STICKER-PICTURE BOOTHS"

IMS PRESIDENT TOMOMI MIKAGE

booths over to sticker-picture booths." Mikage, twenty-seven years old at the time, had just taken the reins of IMS, which was then an electronic devices and computer company called IM Engineering. The company president had a stroke and Mikage, who was in product planning, stepped in. "I couldn't just let products I worked on come to nothing," she recalls. "And I didn't want people to lose their jobs." Mikage convinced the family of the former president to hand over the debt-ridden company. Getting a loan in mid-1990s Japan was hard enough with the banks still reeling from the collapse of the bubble economy, and even harder for a young woman. Mikage pulled together funds from friends and family as well as from her own savings to keep the company afloat. She renamed the company IMS (Interest Making Service) and shifted the company's focus from computer voice-recording devices to arcade games,

IMS HONCHO TOMOMI MIKAGE chucks a yapping brown poodle up on a platform with a green backdrop. She does the same for another. Both animals are wearing doggy diapers with matching sweater vests, and the green-backdropped platform stands next to the pet sticker-picture machine *With Me*. Mikage takes out her cell phone, because unlike regular sticker-picture machines, *With Me* doesn't have a camera. She snaps off a few digital pics and then loads them into the machine via infrared. After that, she selects from different background and frame designs and even creates a flash animation of the pooches, which she then downloads back onto her mobile "Everyone always has their cell phone with them and people like to have pics of their dogs or cats," says Mikage. "So I thought

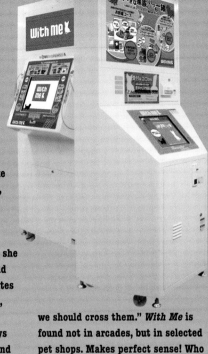

we should cross them." *With Me* is found not in arcades, but in selected pet shops. Makes perfect sense! Who brings their dog to the local game center anyway?

WITH ME: STICKER PICS FOR PETS

phone-card booths, and finally sticker-picture machines. "I was young, naive, and ambitious," she says. "No way I could go through now what I went through then."

High school girls spearheaded the sticker-picture fad. Shoot, most 1990s trends in Japan seemed one way or another to be spawned from teenage girls. From the tanning craze and dyed hair to cell phones and loose socks, these fashionable teenage trendsetters, called "kogals," were always on the cusp, looking for something new, something different. These were the girls that lined up outside arcades like Shibuya's Game Las Vegas to pay three hundred yen for one sheet of sixteen pics—all of the same pic. In comparison, machines

> **"PURIKURA NO MECCA IS WHERE EVERYONE GATHERS, AND THIS IS WHERE ALL THE LATEST MACHINES ARE"**
>
> YOSHIHITO YAMANE

a decade later charged only four hundred yen, and allowed sitters to pose for and pick from multiple pics! At first, Game Las Vegas had only a few sticker-picture machines, but when the management realized that more and more people were using them, booths were moved to the front of the arcade to catch impulse foot traffic, as the sticker-picture trend spread through junior high school kids like a case of mono. By 1996, 70 percent of Atlus' sales were *Print Club*, and parents were just starting to get intrigued. Atlus was no longer known as a game developer, but as the company that gave birth to *Print Club*. "I took my first sticker picture at my local arcade back in 1997 when I was fourteen," says Sakurina. As Japan went bananas for sticker pics, Shibuya's Game Las Vegas went as far as trading out every single arcade cabinet for sticker-picture machines and renaming itself Purikura no Mecca.

Purikura no Mecca sits smack dab in the middle of Center-gai, or Center Street, a stone's throw from Shibuya's scramble crossing

(the world's busiest!). "By Mecca, we meant, you know, 'Mecca,'" points out Yoshihito Yamane, manager of the arcade. "This is where everyone gathers, and this is where all the latest machines are." A group of schoolgirls huddle around a glossy sheet of sticker pictures, fresh out of the machine. The four-by-six-inch sheet features pocket-sized photographs of various dimensions on sticky-backed, glossy paper that can be cut out. The photographic images are covered with add-on flowers, hearts, cutesy characters, and catch phrases. The troop of gals goes over to a nearby circular table and they take turns cutting out their favorite pics from the sheet and putting them in their sticker-picture albums. "I feel so cute when I do purikura," gushes sixteen-year-old Rika Suzuki. "The photographs actually make you look cuter." This is not mere schoolgirl hyperbole: companies like IMS have created software for sticker-picture machines that digitally and instantly makes eyes wider and lips rosy and evenly spaces out eyes, nose, and mouth. Another group of college-aged teens in designer jeans check their makeup before pushing their way into another booth. Boyfriends are lugged in by their girlfriends to take sticker pictures as well. That's all there is to do here, anyway! The entire arcade is crammed wall-to-wall with over a dozen pastel and pink sticker-pic machines, each plastered with images of models dipped in makeup and dripping with saccharine.

Besides being the first sticker-pic specialty arcade in Japan, Purikura no Mecca did another nationwide first: no boys allowed. >>>>>>>>

"Guys are just trying to pick up chicks anyway," points out Sakurina. That means that unless males are with a female patron, they cannot enter the arcade. "That's the rule, but if a group of male patrons is well behaved," adds Yamane, "we don't toss 'em out." In the mid-to-late 1990s with fighting games all the rage, arcades were packed with testosterone. And girls that did frequent game centers were likely to get hit on. "That's one of the reasons we made Purikura no Mecca not just sticker-picture-machine only, but also female only," says Yamane. "Another reason is that we had problems with rude male customers startling girls while they were posing, to deliberately ruin the pictures." Those unhappy sitters then would ask the game center for a refund.

BOYS ARE LUGGED IN BY THEIR GIRLFRIENDS

Why did sticker-picture mania hit so hard? "The appeal is still being able to take pictures with your friends, writing on them together, waiting for them to print, and cutting them out together," reckons Yamane. "At its core, taking sticker pictures is about communication between friends." That, and looking cute. Really, really cute. "Collect one thousand purikura and achieve happiness," was a popular saying in the late 1990s, and gals carted around sticker-picture-filled albums called *purikura cho* (*cho* means notebook in Japanese). Page after page was filled with sticker pictures of friends, friend's friends, random strangers, and random strangers' friends. In the late twentieth century, this was like an analog Facebook. Teens were happy to pose with people they didn't know just to get another sticker picture. Recalls author Hiroko Yoda, a grad student at the time, "They called these people their friends but it kind of weirded me and my buddies out. Like, 'what's wrong with those kids? Don't they realize those aren't really their friends?'" Nope! Groups of gals carrying sticker-picture

name ひぐとも ♡
birthday S61 5 1　type A型
message
よろしくねッ ☆

STICKER PICS ARE ABOUT LOOKING CUTE. REALLY, REALLY CUTE.

albums through the Shibuya streets cause companies to take notice. In 1997, seemingly every arcade-game company (Konami, Taito, and even fighting-game specialist SNK) was churning out sticker-picture machines. While Atlus owns the *Print Club* moniker, other companies called their products "sticker machines" to avoid legal trouble. Names aside, these upstart machines began competing with Atlus for schoolgirl spending money.

Ballpoint-pen scrawl covers the walls at Purikura no Mecca.

"We don't mind if kids write on the walls," says Yamane. "Scribbling is part of doing sticker pictures." The first few incarnations of sticker-picture machines didn't feature the now ubiquitous touchscreen and pen, which let users write funny messages, *rakugaki*, on the pics. So gals did that themselves with magic markers. Realizing the already built-in audience for this scribbling feature, Konami released *Puri Puri Canvas* (1997), which let kids digitally write on their

GRAFFITI IN PURIKURA NO MECCA

pics via an LCD touchscreen and then digitally print out those messages. Competing companies rushed out their own rakugaki versions, and digital drawing became the norm. Atlus' *Super Purikura 21* (1998) included features like spray-paint-type pens for sitters to select from. The touch LCD screen simplified things like selecting and placing frames and various backgrounds on the stickers. By the end of the 1990s, makers had figured out gold, silver, and glitter rakugaki that would sparkle when printed out. In the year 2000, it would dawn on the sticker-picture wizards to include not one but two touch pens at the LCD touchscreen terminal, because people, unless strange, don't take sticker pictures alone. Truly important innovations.

Since the first sticker-picture machine, innovations have been constant. Late 1996 brought the inevitable *Print Club 2* from Atlus, which offered a now standard feature: a privacy curtain. While the prequel had sitters flash cutesy smiles and peace signs in open view, *Print Club 2* let them do that discreetly. The advent of the curtain would also allow the use of a green screen, making CG backgrounds possible. Of course, the curtain would later allow for other, DIY innovations such as take-your-clothes-off sticker pics, aka *eropuri* (erotic purikura). For live-at-home teens, the sticker-picture booth offered

RAKUGAKI START!   RAKUGAKI SCREEN   RAKUGAKI PEN

a chance to escape, be a superstar, and possibly pick up an STD. After booths able to take full-body-length sticker pics were introduced with the machine *Street Snap* (Towa/Hitachi Software, 1998), the trend moved more and more towards fashion-modeling-inspired booths. Machines promised thinner waists and larger busts. Some machines even blew air at the girls as they posed, for that windswept effect! And when Shibuya finally came out of its tanned-to-a-crisp, kogal beach-bunny California dreamin' fantasy at the turn of the millennium, pale skin was in. Girls wanted to look as white as possible. The parasol was the accessory of choice, and the sticker-picture machines were ready to help the fashion conscious achieve the new look. Thank Hitachi Software for that! Its 2002 booth >>>>>>>>

Junshin Bisha (Innocent Heart Beautiful Picture) featured a lighting setup that matched any pro photographer's studio. *Junshin Bisha* offered four different lighting settings that didn't create any shadows on the sitter's face, whitening it, and actually hiding blemishes like acne. Hitachi Software even developed a booth that could give girls virtual hair extensions and retouch makeup. In a country where formal matchmaking is still a popular way to meet a marriage partner, these enhanced sticker pictures would even find their way into the photographic portfolios sent to potential suitors before meeting.

At the height of the sticker-pic craze that swept Japan in the late 1990s, there were twenty-five Purikura no Meccas across the country. The mecca of Purika no Meccas was undoubtedly the branch located at the intersection of all things kawaii: youth-centric Shibuya. "Students on field trips to Tokyo would come here and have their official class

A FASHION-MODELING-INSPIRED BOOTH

pictures, with their teacher and everything, taken in front of the Shibuya Purikura no Mecca," recalls Yamane. That was even if they had a Purikura no Mecca in their hometown! If sticker pictures were this popular in Japan, next stop, America. In 1997, Atlus set up an American arm dedicated to purikura called Atlus Dream Entertainment Co. The company imported two thousand *Print Club* machines into the US, but had sold only four hundred of them by the following year. While the arcade scene was thriving in Japan, it was dead as dead in America. Atlus couldn't figure out where to put them, and Americans couldn't figure out what the hell these *Print Club* machines were. "It's a pain to insert three dollar's worth

STICKER PICS ARE ABOUT COMMUNICATION BETWEEN FRIENDS

of change when the largest denomination is a quarter, and so business was difficult," says Atlus's Hiraoka. "However, in some malls
and shops, particularly in Las Vegas, it did have some success."
Atlus threw in the towel, returned to Japan, and focused again on
what originally made Atlus: games.

In Japan, the sticker-picture industry was at an impasse. Machines
continued to produce better- and better-looking pictures, but beyond
that, makers seemed to be at a loss. Innovation came to mean adding poles or sofas or subway-car-style handle straps for posing. Sega
tried introducing *videokura*, which created video clips that could be
downloaded onto cell phones, but that didn't exactly set Shibuya
on fire. IMS is looking into expanding sticker-picture machines into
China—not just into the country's game centers and but also into
restaurants, where couples on dates can snap pics. IMS has also
released a sticker-picture machine for pets called *With Me*, which
is proving popular. "There are fewer kids these days," points out ⟫⟫⟫⟫⟫⟫⟫⟫⟫

SEND THE PHOTO TO YOUR CELL PHONE

Purikura no Mecca's Yamane. "The population of Japan is decreasing." Fewer kids means fewer customers. Purikura no Mecca has seen its empire of specialty arcades dwindle to eight. With sticker-picture machines costing game centers the same as a mid-sized car at over twenty thousand US dollars (and way more to develop), companies had a hard time justifying the expense in a shrinking market. By late 2007, it was possible to count sticker machine makers on one hand. Former sticker-picture giant Hitachi Software had long since stepped out, and the genre's founder Atlus seemed to be releasing obligatory machines only because it had the name *Print Club* trademarked. Another factor, according to Yamane, is that private schools do not permit students to wear their uniforms after school. So, typically, private school kids go straight home after school and change clothes, instead of shopping and hanging out with friends. Failure to do so could mean being reprimanded if seen still in uniform by other classmates, teachers, or parents. "Lots of kids don't feel like going back outside after getting home," Yamane adds. And there's something else too. "This," says Yamane, taking out his cell phone. Not so much the cell phone itself, but the digital camera on it.

Camera phones hit Japan in large numbers in late 2001. Early models took grainy one-megapixel photographs and featured small mirrors next to the camera lens so users could see themselves for self-portraits. Keeping with the times, Atlus and other makers offered networked sticker-picture machines that printed out URLs on the actual sheets of stickers, which needed to be entered into the phone's Internet browser. Obviously, with phones still unable to support hi-res images, there was a significant decline in quality. Sticker pictures had a tremendous edge in clarity. Though, as camera phones approached three, four, and five megapixels, the gap closed. "A lot of kids today don't carry around sticker-picture albums," Yamane says. "Machines now make it possible to download hi-res pictures directly from the booth to cell phones. Most kids have their sticker pictures on their phones." The one advantage that sticker-picture booths still have is that they make it possible to cram five or six people into one picture. "Yeah, some girls might prefer using camera phones, but not me," says Sakurina, looking at her faux-jewel-encrusted cell phone. "Sticker pics all the way." ✿

ANOTHER DIMENSION

Putting pictures on stickers? Great idea. Putting sticker pictures on, say, business cards? Hrm. In an effort to appeal to salarymen, Atlus rolled out *Business Purikura* in late 1997. Designed to print out small sticker pics for business cards, the machine was equipped with a Kodak digital camera for headshots and had a memory-card slot so that company logos could be added! Electronics maker Sanyo did one better than simple business card stickers with *Pierimo* (2001), first located in the company's Internet café, a service that's sadly no longer available. This 3-D modeling system could snap off a bunch of photos to produce a likeness of the subject in the form of a statue. Once inside the blue-screened *Pierimo* booth, twenty-eight cameras would map your face in approximately three seconds. The 3-D polygon data was then sent to the hard drive, and relayed to a factory. An off-site rotating drill then produced a sculpture made from artificial polyurethane resin, which was mailed to the customer a week later. *Pierimo*'s popularity spread throughout Korea and China as well as Japan—after all, who could resist a cute, key-chain-sized statue in their own image for only three thousand yen? Or a life-size doppelgänger for two million yen? Sure beats stickers!

SALARYMAN STATUES

MUSIC
BLARING,
BODIES
MOVING.

This is gaming at two hundred beats per minute. Go to the rhythm section of any Japanese arcade, and you'll smell it: sweat. A towel and a change of shirt is a must, not to mention a bottle of water. These music-based games literally stand apart from the rows of sedentary game cabinets. These games get players up off their duffs. They get players to move.

It's a week night, but the Brunswick Sports Garden, in Tokyo's Ikebukuro district, is packed. The upper stories house a pool hall, a bowling alley, and a batting cage, but the second floor is a game center with an entire section dedicated to music games. "The arcades in central Tokyo districts like Akihabara and Shinjuku tend to charge two hundred yen," says Canadian player Aaron Chmielowiec, a longtime resident of Japan, "but nobody who is serious pays over a hundred yen, except in a pinch." Aaron feeds his Konami e-amusement pass, a IC-chip embedded smart card, into a *DanceDanceRevolution SuperNOVA 2* cabinet. The card saves his online rankings, and his first name

THESE GAMES GET PLAYERS TO MOVE

pops up on the screen. "I always register my name the first day games hit the arcades," he says. "Even if there aren't that many Aarons in Japan."

Around Aaron, a cacophony of musical sounds blares out. A guy in a Paul Smith shirt shreds through guitar sim *GuitarFreaks*, while a twenty-something woman in a skirt and leggings pounds DJ rhythm game *beatmania IIDX 15 DJ TROOPERS* like she's typing. Schoolgirls cluster around cutesy *pop'n music*, their school sweaters tied around their waists, slapping brightly colored buttons as corresponding ones appear on screen. After the players finish the sets, they get back in the line formed behind each cabinet, waiting to feed the machine more coins. This cycle, like a record spinning around and around, continues for the rest of the evening. Others simply stand and marvel. "Playing these rhythm arcade games is like a performance for everyone in the arcade," explains musician and game developer Masaya Matsuura, who designed some of the first music games, like PlayStation title *PaRappa the Rapper* (1996).

One of the few Japanese game-center titles to have made the leap to Western arcades in a big way since *Street Fighter II* is *Dance-DanceRevolution*, or *DDR*, which continues to get US and European releases even though it was first introduced back in 1998. It's a cornerstone of game-maker Konami's Bemani brand, which is dedicated exclusively to music-based titles. The concept is simple:

PERFECT! PERFECT! MARVELOUS! FLASH ON THE SCREEN AS AARON STOMPS OUT DDR SUPERNOVA 2

players step on pressure-sensitive pads in the order dictated by on-screen arrows. Doing so successfully fills their energy bar. Failing to do so drains it. The basic idea might be simple, but doing it is another matter. The scrolling on-screen songs can have over six hundred steps and last several minutes. It's physically exhausting! The arcade versions aren't nearly as forgiving as the home-console ones, and the demanding patterns get harder year after year.

Perfect! Perfect! Marvelous! flash on the screen as Aaron stomps out *DDR SuperNOVA 2*. *Marvelous!* is a hair better than *Perfect!* Aaron's racking up both. Techno music blasts from the neon speakers, and Aaron, decked out in a soccer jersey, does a series of rapid steps. The guy in the Paul Smith shirt has moved from *GuitarFreaks* to *DDR* and is now on the machine next to Aaron. This guy looks more like he's actually dancing. His movement are very fluid and ornate, complete with spin turns and hand gestures. Aaron looks like he's playing a game.

There are two styles of *DDR* play. Those like the guy in the Paul Smith shirt are putting on a show. It's much easier to dance when the game's on its lowest difficulty level. Then there are those like >>>>>>>>

Aaron, who are pushing their bodies to the limit, and attempting to complete seemingly impossible songs on the highest difficulty setting. The emphasis isn't on style, but on perfection. His timing is spot on and he scores nothing but *Perfect!* and *Marvelous!* Aaron grabs the cabinet's support bar and continues to nail every arrow. The support bar reduces the player's physical stress (at the expense of limiting the range of movement), freeing him up to hit the arrows with greater precision. "There's some disagreement about using the bar," Aaron later says. "In the West, it's looked down upon, but not so much in Japan. There's nothing in the rules that say players can't use the bar, and most players don't really care either way." The song finishes, and Aaron's "Dance Points" are tallied up. He gets AAA, the highest rank.

"ONE OF THE FACTORS FOR THE POPULARITY OF BEATMANIA IS THAT THE PLAYER LOOKS COOL"

The first installment of the *DDR* series—called simply *Dance-DanceRevolution*—appeared in Japan at the end of 1998. To attract players to a nascent genre, *DDR* featured cover versions of well-known tracks from artists like Olivia Newton John and KC & The Sunshine Band. The dance patterns were relatively simple, and *DDR* was a smash hit. *DDR* wasn't the first music-based arcade game from developer Konami. The first was *beatmania*, a rhythm-style DJ-ing game in 1997. "When we developed the concept of a game centered on music we knew we wanted to create something cool," says a Konami staffer. "We brainstormed ideas and came up with a game where the player is a DJ." Konami wasn't sure if the game would take off in Japanese game centers, where players were used to sitting down. *Beatmania* had players stand on a stage, press buttons laid out like a piano, and scratch a rubber record. In short, they pretended they were club DJs. "Japanese do not like to stand out, and they tend to be shy," adds Konami. "So we were worried if people would accept this game style." The game was a surprise hit, and Konami's Games & Music Division changed its name to Bemani in honor of that game. Says Konami: "We think one of the factors for the popularity of *beatmania* is that the player looks cool."

PLAYER 3

NAME: **AARON CHMIELOWIEC**
SPECIALTY: **RHYTHM GAMES**
FAVORITE GAME: **DANCE DANCE REVOLUTION**

Meet Aaron Chmielowiec. By day, he's an IT manager at a Tokyo media corporation. By night, a dancing machine.

Aaron first came to Japan from his native Canada when he was still a university student, after getting an internship with Seiko Epson, and is now a long-term resident. The first time he stepped on a *DDR* machine was Halloween 1998. It was the first installment in the *DDR* series, *DanceDanceRevolution*, which found its way to the Japan Alps city of Nagano, where Aaron then lived. Aaron, who grew up playing arcade games, had never seen or played anything like it. "The game felt intuitive," he recalls. "It was like the electronic game *Simon* for your feet. There was a logic to it."

By 1999, when *DDR 3rdMIX* came out, Aaron was hooked. He befriended the core Tokyo players and set up a website (http://aaronin.jp/) that catalogued *DDR* scores, first hands-on (feet-on?) game impressions, and pictures of buddies tearing up the pads. Aaron began posting his own scores, including a host of AAAs—a score rarely achieved by Western gamers

at the time. "People on the Internet thought those pictures were phony," he says. "At that time, they thought there was no way someone could get an AAA." In an age before YouTube, Aaron uploaded video clips of himself and his friends getting perfect scores, which converted some non-believers. "My site was also breaking news, like soundtrack listings for new Bemani games."

Gaming for Aaron didn't start with *DDR*. He likes to tell the story of the time when, as a young boy, he memorized the algorithms in *Pac-Man* and crashed the game at his local Canadian arcade after getting to the game's 256th level. Is the ability to memorize patterns the key to his *DDR* success? He shrugs. "You just need to think about the song's rhythm, and how you're supposed to step," he says, modestly.

While he plays, Aaron bobs his head as he counts off the beats. Passersby stop to check out what exactly this foreign dude is doing on the pads. "The fact that there are people watching makes these arcade rhythm games similar to an actual musical performance," points out Masaya Matsuura. He should know. Before he began creating music games for home consoles, Matsuura was the leader of Japanese synth-pop band PSY·S. "The difference is that playing these games costs money, while musicians earn money. Plus, players don't need an understanding of music or arrangement." Tone deaf and uncoordinated players will find these rhythm titles frustrating, however. Unlike Matsuura, Aaron believes an understanding of music helps. Studying karate in Japan taught him how to move, but studying classical piano and trumpet helped Aaron understand how to groove.

Beatmania proved there was a market for these music-based rhythm games. Konami rolled out a slew of arcade titles in 1998 and 1999: guitar simulator *GuitarFreaks*, drum simulator *DrumMania*, button-pressing rhythm title *pop'n music*, and *Dance-*

DIGITAL DANCING

For a game based on dancing, *Dance Dance Revolution* has made the jump to PCs. And so have its clones. With names like *Flash Flash Revolution* or *Delight Delight Reduplication*, the copycat versions ditch the foot pad for the computer's arrow keys. Computer peripheral manufacturers have even churned out mini type pads that can be hooked up to your computer's USB port to let your fingers do the dancing!

"THE FACT THAT THERE ARE PEOPLE WATCHING MAKES THESE ARCADE RHYTHM GAMES SIMILAR TO AN ACTUAL MUSICAL PERFORMANCE"

MASAYA MATSUURA

DanceRevolution—all of them establishing themselves as strong arcade franchises. The games were unlike anything gamers had ever seen. "Before the release of *beatmania*, most games were played using a joystick," explains a Konami staffer. "And driving simulators were based on things like driving cars, gun shooting games on firing guns, or boxing games on punching things." Bemani's output was new, fresh, and different from the standard arcade fare.

Japan was ready to boogie. In the late 1990s, arcade owners moved the *DDR* machines onto the sidewalk, where pedestrians could watch players dance. "*DDR* was so big that even my local coin laundromat had a machine," says Aaron. "Some people went there to wash clothes, but more went to play *DDR*." By the time *DDR 3rdMIX* came out in 1999, gamers were lining up around the block to play. Guys were dragging along their girlfriends to show off their dancing skills. At that time, arcade owners could even charge players two hundred yen for two songs, more than double the going rate ten years later. Still, *DDR*-hungry gamers gladly forked it over.

DDR went supernova abroad as well. While *beatmania*'s pretend-you're-a-DJ stylings weren't to American tastes (Europeans lapped it up), the idea of jumping around on pressure-sensitive pads to cheesy techno music was. "The game really helped introduce that style of dance music to a lot of people in America," ▸▸▸▸▸▸▸▸

says Aaron. A series of CDs with music from Bemani games was released by Toshiba EMI. In-house composers also lent their musical talents, creating original tracks for the series. For example, the composer of the eerie soundtrack for Konami's horror series *Silent Hill*—a console game and also a Hollywood movie—also created funky beats for *beatmania IIDX*. A Konami staffer sheds light on how music is selected: "Everyone has different tastes. So we include a variety of music in each game. This also gives people a chance to hear music that they wouldn't otherwise listen to."

With the Bemani coffers overflowing, Konami was willing to chance it with new types of games. The Bemani division churned out an array of music-based games to see what stuck. *Pop'n music*, the cute and deceptively difficult version of *beatmania* with colorful buttons, did. The *DDR*-aping

ONE OF THE MOST SUCCESSFUL OF ALL THE ARCADE GAMES INSPIRED BY THE MUSIC BOOM WAS TAIKO NO TATSUJIN

version called *pop'n stage* (1999) didn't. Nor did keyboard simulator *KeyboardMania* (2000). Then there was the misfire *DanceManiax* (2000), which was similar to *beatmania*, but had players move their hands through invisible sensor beams instead of pressing buttons. *ParaParaParadise* (2000) also had players move their hands under sensors, in the style of late-nineties dance craze *para para*. (Think Japanese teens with bleached hair line-dancing to trashy techno tunes, while waving their arms around in intricate, predetermined moves.) These sensor-based games had players struggle to follow unnecessarily complex dance moves with their hands.

Bemani's success brought a host of imitators. *DanceDance-Revolution* alone saw more than ten copycats in game centers and on consoles, including Korean arcade clone *Pump It Up* and American arcade title *In The Groove*. Both games had a game mechanic suspiciously similar to *DDR*—stepping on arrows in tangent with on-screen ones. *In The Groove* had four arrow pads, while *Pump It Up* had five. Andamiro, the Korean developer behind *Pump It Up*, first learned about *DDR* at the Amusement Machine Show in Tokyo in fall 1998. By the next year, it had copied the concept and released *Pump It Up*. The game looked like *DDR* and played like *DDR*. No wonder Konami took the Korean company to court, and the Seoul District Court ruled in Konami's favor.

TAIKO NO TATSUJIN

Konami also filed an intellectual property lawsuit against *In The Groove*'s developer Roxor Games and through this litigation successfully acquired the intellectual property rights to *In The Groove*.

One of the most successful of all the arcade games inspired by the music boom was *Taiko no Tatsujin* (2001) from developer Namco (now Namco Bandai Games Inc.). The title translates as "Drum Master" and the cabinet features two large traditional Japanese drums, or *taiko*. Players bang out patterns in time with scrolling music taken from a variety of pop songs. The game and its cute drum characters Katsu and Don—whose names are a wordplay on the sound a Japanese drum makes as well as the name of the Japanese pork dish *katsudon*—immediately appealed to the Japanese sensibility. >>>>>>>

"I think that because *Taiko no Tatsujin* mixes two elements that are well-known to all Japanese—the traditional drum and contemporary pop music—and because the drum is so easy and fun to play, the game was a hit with a wide range of players," says Ken Nakadate, who planned the first *Taiko no Tatsujin*. While Bemani games had players pretend that they are playing instruments, *Taiko no Tatsujin* actually has mock drums for the gamers to play. "Since we designed the game so that players could experience the fun of Japanese drums without real technique, we don't know if the game actually improves players' real drumming skills," says Nakadate. "Though I did hear about one guy who got interested in Japanese drums through *Taiko no Tatsujin* and started learning how to play the taiko." Real drumming or not, there's a festival atmosphere to the game, and it's not surprising to see nerd herds dancing in formation (they're known as *otagei*—otaku performers) while a "drum master" pounds out a cute J-pop tune.

It was around the time *DDR 3rdMIX* came out in 1999 that the diehard players started coming into their own. As players improved, new versions of the games became more difficult. "If you compared the first *DDR* to the *5thMIX*, which came out less than two years later, you could see how much harder the game was getting," says Aaron. "The first mix wasn't that hard, but that was because nobody had played it before." The game eased players in and wasn't intimidating for casual folks. But as players got better and better, subsequent mixes became harder and harder. Likewise, *beatmania*

ROCK BAND

SETUP

SELECT ROCKER

Back

also got an update in 2000 with *beatmania IIDX*, which featured a rubber turntable and had seven buttons instead of five. The song scrolls got longer and the patterns got increasingly challenging. For *DDR*, Konami even introduced a new scoring category: *Marvelous!* which was higher than *Perfect!* The timing window to hit *Marvelous!* is far smaller, making the game challenging for the most seasoned players. Says Aaron, "Barring the easiest of songs, I've never seen anyone clear a stage with all *Marvelous!*"

DDR has a one-player mode, with four arrows to follow, or a two-player mode. Two-player mode scrolls eight arrows on the screen, four for each player. Aaron's playing the two-player mode. By himself. That means he's contending with eight on-screen arrows and eight footpads. "Sometimes it's hard to know where your body is supposed to move," he says. The noise in the game center is deafening, the music from each cabinet drowning out the one next to it. Says Alex Rigopulos, CEO of developer Harmonix Music Systems: "From a >>>>>>>

THE NOISE IN THE GAME CENTER IS DEAFENING. THE MUSIC FROM EACH CABINET DROWNING OUT THE ONE NEXT TO IT

ALEX RIGOPULOS, CEO OF HARMONIX MUSIC SYSTEMS

purely auditory standpoint, this is just about the worst environment imaginable to try to enjoy a music game."

In Japan, the arcades were the only option for this genre. "Selling big custom peripherals for loud music games into small Japanese homes in crowded neighborhoods wasn't really feasible, so the arcades were the path of least resistance," points out Rigopulos. He should know. His company Harmonix is capitalizing on music games geared for Western markets. With smash hit console games *Guitar Hero* and *Rock Band*, the Boston-based developer is responsible for taking arcade-style music games and successfully putting them in Western living rooms. And since the consoles are jacked into the Internet, Harmonix is able to sell players a steady stream of new song downloads in a business model that Konami's Bemani division could only dream of.

Before Harmonix hit it big with *Guitar Hero* and *Rock Band* in 2005 and 2007, the developer worked on Konami Bemani title *Karaoke Revolution* for the PlayStation 2. Arcade cabinets were outfitted with special PlayStation 2 memory card slots so gamers could play their saved PS2 games at the arcade. Still, with the PS2 keeping more and more gamers at home, Konami released home versions of its Bemani games. Doing so opened up the titles to an audience who were perhaps too shy to try out the games in the game center. *DDR* for the PS2 was bundled with a vinyl mat. "It's much more forgiving than the arcade

HEAVENLY BEATS

Here's the way it traditionally goes: game is released in arcades and then ported to home and portable consoles. If that's the way it usually goes down, *Rhythm Tengoku* (2006) is an anomaly. The game is one of the last that Nintendo designed specifically for its portable Game Boy Advance hardware platform before shifting one hundred percent to the newer Nintendo DS. *Rhythm Tengoku*, which translates as "Rhythm Heaven," is a straight-up music game where players press buttons in time with on-screen prompts. In an unorthodox move, Nintendo decided to rope in former home-console rival Sega to put out a *Rhythm Tengoku* arcade port. The arcade cabinet even features Nintendo's iconic directional pad and A and B buttons. It's as if the Game Boy Advance has been magnified by a hundred!

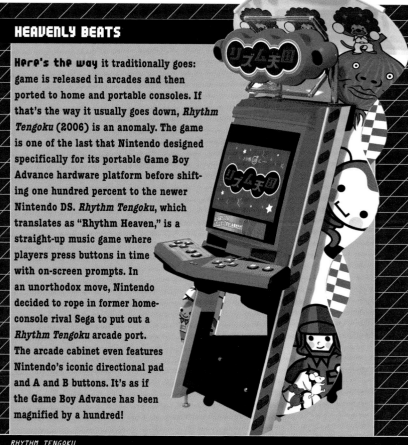

RHYTHM TENGOKU

version and much easier to score *Perfect!* on it," says Aaron. To compensate for the poor quality of the home pads, DIY types even constructed steel *DDR* pads for home use. Some even illuminated them with neon lights.

Even in 2001 and 2002, *DDR* fans were still frequenting the game centers—although in dwindling numbers. Home versions of *DDR* started hitting consoles in mid-1999, but the arcade cabinets ensured greater precision than the home counterparts. A dichotomy began: hard-core players sweated it out in the game center, while casual players played watered-down home versions like *Dance Dance Revolution: Mario Mix* (2005). "The result is that the arcade versions are dominated by these incredible hard-core virtuosi, playing outrageously difficult patterns," says Alex Rigopulos. "This is really intimidating for curious newcomers."

DDR on home consoles brought the game a new audience: health nuts. "After the PlayStation version of *DDR* came out," says a Konami staffer, "celebrities in Japan began to tell journalists that the *DDR* games helped them lose weight in an enjoyable way." Japanese consumers snapped up the home version, hoping to drop a few pounds. Aaron, meanwhile, was getting down in Tokyo game centers. "In the first year I played, I lost over sixty pounds," he says. Konami, who also owns a chain of fitness clubs in Japan, wasn't surprised—staffers lost weight while testing the game series. *DDR* became known as exercise equipment abroad as well. In 2007, California governor Arnold Schwarzenegger pushed the home version into schools in an effort to promote fitness. The game was even deemed acceptable as a university Physical Education credit.

It's late. The players at the Brunswick Sports Garden don't show any sign of slowing down. They just keep going. Plastic fans sit in front of the cabinets, spinning cool air. Songs continue to scroll on screens. The guy in the Paul Smith shirt pounds drums on *Drum-Mania*, the schoolgirls keep hitting the *pop'n music* buttons, and a woman in a hat tickles plays two-player *beatmania* by herself. It feels less like a game center and more like a gym. "We're lucky to have games that inspire physical action," says Aaron, wiping his brow. Yes, yes we are.

GAMING IS GOOD FOR YOU

Think video games are bad for kids? Think again. In 2006, the state of West Virginia, which has one of the highest rates of childhood obesity in the US, announced plans to incorporate *DDR* into the curriculum of all 765 of their public schools. The idea came about after a professor from the Motor Development Center at West Virginia University saw kids pounding the dance pads in an arcade, sweating like crazy, and quenching their thirst with gallons of water. A scientific study into the health benefits of the game came up with the startling results that this was indeed a healthy way for the nation's youth to spend its time. Konami agreed to team up with state-based agencies to supply schools with Xbox game consoles, dance pads, and software. Best school supplies ever!

THEY'RE CALLED BULLET HELL FOR GOOD REASON.

Shoot 'em ups or "shmups" typically feature a sole aircraft flying into a bullet hailstorm. Each spray of brightly colored pellets is a pattern gamers must memorize. In difficult games like *DonPachi* or *Batsugun*, bullets fill the screen, and the player's ship is a few pixels. They must maneuver through micro-sized openings in the bullet patterns to avoid death. Shmup players need quick reactions, brains, and guts.

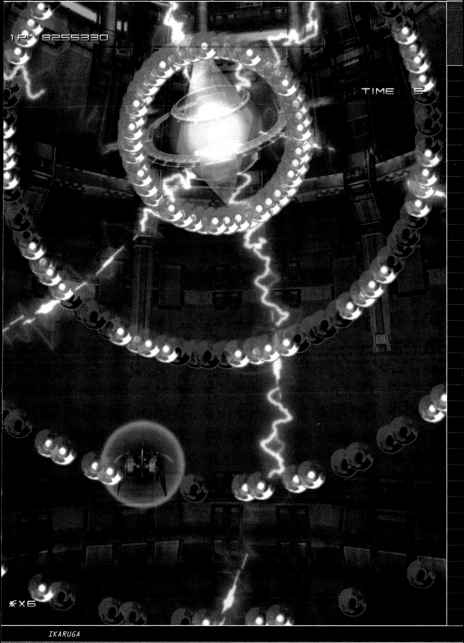

AKIHABARA TAITO HEY

SHMUP HEAVEN

>>>>>>>>>>> In a smoky corner of Taito Hey, an arcade in Tokyo nerd haven Akihabara with over sixty shoot 'em up games, a heavy salaryman with saggy black socks guides planes through a blaze of bullets. The entire upright screen is literally covered in ammo. He taps the joystick in sudden, jerky reflex movements. This is exactly why these games are called "twitch shooters." Split-second decisions are being made, and beads of sweat collect on brows as cool air-conditioning circulates. Behind the salaryman, two lanky teens lurk. They're not waiting, but watching. Saggy-socks unloads a hail of fire, destroying an enormous demonic enemy boss in a ball of flames.

Want to visit the best place for shooting games in the world? Taito Hey is it. "People don't come here to practice," amateur shmup maker Kenta Cho says. "They practice elsewhere and come here to play." The floor is filled with cabinets dedicated to shooting games, aka "STG" in Japan. Shmup heaven! The arcade manager, who's been working at Hey since 2005, confesses, "I dig shooters. I'm not good at them but I still dig them." The regulars have their favorite games, but are most likely to shoot up

"PEOPLE DON'T COME HERE TO PRACTICE. THEY COME HERE TO PLAY."

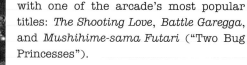

KENTA CHO TAKES ON *IKARUGA*

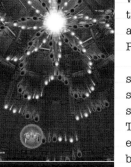

IKARUGA

with one of the arcade's most popular titles: *The Shooting Love*, *Battle Garegga*, and *Mushihime-sama Futari* ("Two Bug Princesses").

Putting down his black backpack, Cho stuffs a hundred-yen coin into a cabinet, selects the hardest difficulty level, and starts playing a shooter called *Ikaruga* by Treasure Co., Ltd. While this game isn't exactly new (*Ikaruga* hit Japanese arcades back in late 2001), it does show that the genre has long evolved from the straight-forward shooters of the early 1980s. "The game that's influenced me the most is *Ikaruga*," gushes Tsuneki Ikeda, chief programmer at shmup specialty developer Cave. "It really impacted me on many different levels, and I've gotten a lot of inspiration from it." The graphics still hold up, and it's hard to believe the postapocalyptic game was created by a four-man team. Tiny! Typically, hundreds of people will work on a big budget console game. >>>>>>>>>>

Cruising through the innards of some futuristic space station, two bullet streams cascade towards his spacecraft: one stream is red and black, the other is blue and white. Tapping a button, Cho's ship flips over and changes color from white to black, absorbing the dark slugs without dying, and dodging the lethal light-colored ones. Suddenly, white bullets pour down, and Cho switches his spaceship to white, absorbing those bullets. The game is methodical, and a calculating Cho toggles back and forth, flipping his craft between the white and black polarities. Enemies appear from the top and bottom of

CHO CLEARS THE STAGE AND PROCEEDS TO THE NEXT,WHERE A REDDISH ENEMY WITH FOUR PODLIKE CANNONS RELENTLESSLY FIRES BULLETS

IKARUGA

the screen, attacking from both directions. Black fighters appear, followed by white ones, both spraying bullets at Cho, who's blasting his way through, making the enemies explode like popcorn. He clears the stage and proceeds to the next, where a reddish enemy with four podlike cannons relentlessly fires bullets. If that wasn't enough, there are laser beams. Eight laser beams. Flames engulf the screen.

Hard-core, but Cho doesn't consider himself a top player (called a "scorer" in Japanese). By day, the thirty-something bi-speckled researcher works at a major Japanese electronics company, doing multimedia R&D. By night, he is ABA Games, a one-man freeware PC game-design company famous for its avant-garde reimagining of arcade shooters. "A shmup is a good playground to try new game features," Cho says. New features may be easy to implement, but it's difficult to stand out from other shooters. Genre conventions dictate that a shoot 'em up consists of a craft at a fixed position, shooting enemies and dodging bullets. That convention,

PLAYER 5

NAME: **KENTA CHO**
SPECIALTY: **SHOOTERS**
FAVORITE GAME: **IKARUGA**

Kenta Cho has been called one of the best independent programmers in the world. As a kid in the early 1980s, he started writing code for his first microcomputer, an NEC PC-6001. "It was perfectly natural to make games when I was young," he says, "because there were so few titles on the market." After university Cho flirted with the idea of joining Sega as a game developer. But what he really wanted to do was research, and he ended up joining Toshiba, where he works in R&D. He still makes games as a hobby, and cranks out a new downloadable game about once every six months or so. What's more, he's even written an open-source PC program called BulletML that can replicate bullet barrages from classic shooters like *Xevious*. "I'm trying to keep creating one game every six months," he says, "but recently it tends to take more time." Best known for games *Gunroar* and *Tumiki Fighters*, his freeware games are downloaded all over the world via his website (http://www.asahi-net.or.jp/~cs8k-cyu/index_e.html), which also has an English page. In the West, he's hailed as the most famous "*doujin* software" shmup maker. Doujin games are created by hobbyists (think fangames), are typically sold at doujin conventions like Tokyo's biannual Comiket, and usually rework or pay homage to well-known games, anime, and manga. "I guess abroad I'm known as a doujin software creator, and that's okay," says Cho. "But I don't sell my games." In Japan, Cho would actually be considered a freeware game maker as his games are completely open-source and, well, free. Why freeware? "If you want to make games," he explains, "it's the easiest and best way. You can reach more people, too." American video-game publisher Majesco Entertainment even ported his *Tumiki Fighters* to the Nintendo Wii. And how much did Cho receive? "Nothing. It's a freeware game after all."

Cho explains, is one reason why making freeware arcade shooters is appealing. "I can focus attention on gameplay and think deeply about how I can invent a new feature," he tells us. "Another reason is, of course, I like to play shmups."

In the 1960s, all computer game programmers were amateurs, like Cho. The first shoot 'em up—the first computer game in fact—was also a hobby-created game. Dubbed *Spacewar!*, the title was created back in 1961 in the United States by Massachusetts Institute of Technology (MIT) computer scientists to amuse fellow lab rats. The game was programmed on a refrigerator-sized computer, and the controllers were built from spare telephone parts. Inspired by the Cold War space race, the premise was simple: two rival spacecraft dogfight, while avoiding hitting a sun. With arcades a decade away, the open-source code was passed around computer labs in universities across the country. When the American arcade scene exploded in the early- to mid-

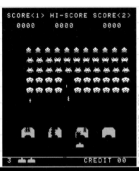

SPACE INVADERS

1970s, fueled by early Atari titles like *Pong* and *Breakout*, *Spacewar!* was even remade into an arcade title—four times. It wasn't until later, though, that players got their first true arcade shooter. The game was called *Space Invaders*. The year was 1978. Its creator, Tomohiro Nishikado of Taito Corporation, was Japanese.

The black-and-white *Space Invaders* featured a movable laser cannon that blasted invading aliens, which approached faster and faster as the music quickened until reaching a frantic pace. The game was challenging, but not impossibly hard. Previous arcade titles had players play against a countdown clock, but *Space Invaders* offered a novelty: players had three lives. Those who got good at the game could play for as long as they could keep from being blown to bits. The game kept looping, so if you were good, you could play as far as your coin would take you.

Compared to the technology used by the MIT researchers in the 1960s to make *Spacewar!*, the programming tools Nishikado had at his disposal in the late 1970s were cutting edge. Compared to today, Nishikado was making games in the Dark Ages. Development was a process of trial and error. "The development of *Space Invaders* took all my energy," recalls Nishikado. Early microprocessors made it impossible to get rendered enemy aircraft to move smoothly. Graphics were herky-jerky, so Nishikado switched out humans for planes. That worked much better, but shooting humans? "Top Taito management decided that killing people was morally wrong, so we ditched that," Nishikado says. "Instead, we changed the humans to space aliens. Problem solved." The octopus-shaped invaders were inspired by H. G. Wells' *The War of the Worlds* and have become so iconic that a French street artist has taken the pseudonym "Invader" and pastes up instantly recognizable mini-invader tile mosaics on buildings, bridges, and other structures in cities all over the world.

The first version released in Japan wasn't even color, but the >>>>>>>

SPACE INVADERS' CREATOR TOMOHIRO NISHIKADO (ABOVE). EARLY "INVADER HOUSE" (BELOW)

SPACE INVADERS WAS SO POPULAR THAT IT CAUSED A NATIONAL YEN COIN SHORTAGE

game captivated the country. With Japan in the throes of *Star Wars* fever, *Space Invaders* was a no-brain arcade smash hit. When players went to arcades, all they wanted to do was shoot aliens in space. It was no accident that the first game centers were called "invader house" in Japanese. They were wall-to-wall with upright and counter-top *Space Invaders* coin-ops. In 1978, these one-room arcades popped up overnight in urban centers like Tokyo and Osaka, blasting out the

game's instantly recognizable "dun dun dun" theme music. *Space Invaders* was so popular that it actually caused a national hundred-yen coin shortage. More shooters followed: the next year saw *Galaxian*, a multicolored shooter with kamikaze enemies, and in 1981, *Galaga*, featuring enemies with tractor beams. Both games were from Namco (now Namco Bandai Games Inc.). Even Nintendo, then known as a

"IN THOSE DAYS, YOU COULD ONLY MAKE A BLACK BACKGROUND, THAT'S WHY THE SETTING WAS SPACE"

GALAXIAN

toy and playing-card maker, produced three *Space Invaders* clones. Nintendo would eventually find its own gaming voice with *Donkey Kong* in 1981, and then with its game consoles.

Space Invaders was a perfect intersection of public taste and available technology. "In those days, with the limited hardware technology available, you could only make a black background, and you couldn't make scrolling shooters. That's why the setting was space," explains game designer Masanobu Endo, formerly of Namco, for whom he designed *Xevious*, a game that took shooting games out of space and put them in the real world. *Xevious*, made in 1982, ran on advanced hardware, making it possible to create a smoothly scrolling terrestrial setting. *Xevious* was like nothing game centers or players had seen. The vertical scrolling levels depicted a real world, with shaded terrain. For its time, the title sported eye-popping graphics. Like the game's predecessors, *Xevious* was a smash

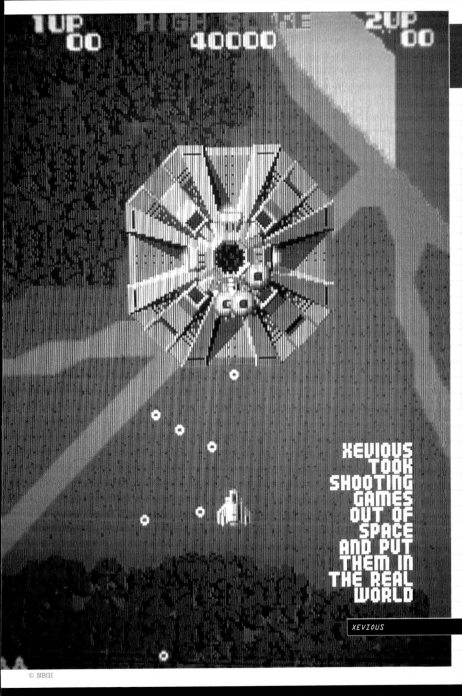

XEVIOUS
TOOK
SHOOTING
GAMES
OUT OF
SPACE
AND PUT
THEM IN
THE REAL
WORLD

XEVIOUS

in Japan, but only a cult hit in the West. These early shooters were immediately approachable for new players. "You don't have to explain the rules," says Endo. Just dodge and shoot, dodge and shoot.

Then things started to get complex. And hard. Really, really hard. In the mid-1980s, side-scrolling *Gradius*, from Konami, introduced a variety of levels—all totally different. While a new player could get relatively far in *Space Invaders* or *Xevious* based on raw skill alone, *Gradius* (and its sequels) wasn't as forgiving. Players were forced to memorize the layout of each level, and the only way to do that was to die repeatedly. More methodical shooting games appeared, based on calculated movements and patterns. While *Space Invaders* rewarded quick reflexes, *Gradius* favored rote memorization and repeat play. You want to beat that game? Start practicing—in other words, feeding the machine coins.

MASANOBU ENDO

DEVIOUS XEVIOUS

Xevious creator and former Namco employee Masanobu Endo was one of the first Japanese game designers to think of himself as more than a nameless programmer—rather a creator. While current game designers are approaching rock star status, the industry's pioneers weren't even allowed to put their name on the game. But Endo left a hidden signature on his creation: at the beginning of the game, move your craft to the right side, and start bombing and shooting. A message appears on the screen:

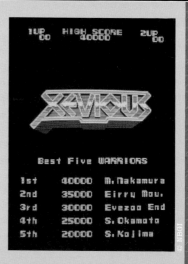

| 1UP | HIGH SCORE | 2UP |
| DO | 40000 | DO |

XEVIOUS

Best Five WARRIORS

1st	40000	M. Nakamura
2nd	35000	Eirry Mou.
3rd	30000	Evezoo End
4th	25000	S. Okamota
5th	20000	S. Kojima

The early 1990s saw a new breed of Japanese shooters, called "maniac shooters." With 3-D games all the rage, 2-D shmup developers thought the best way to dazzle players would be to overwhelm them. Playing relentless shooters like *Batsugun* from Toaplan, and *Battle Garegga* and *DonPachi* from Cave, was like getting a drink from a fire hydrant. The bullets literally rained down on players, whose split-second reactions would decide whether they'd live or die. The games that followed were hard to a point where playing them was daunting. "Hard-core fans of a particular arcade genre get better and better as the sequels come out," Kenta Cho says, "and the difficulty of these sequels becomes higher and higher to adapt to the skills of the players. I can still play shmups released this year, but I can't play fighting games and rhythm games released this century—they are too difficult for those not familiar with those genres."

To please the hard-core players, developers have forsaken the casual players—and even the founding fathers of the various genres. On his days off, *Space Invaders* designer Nishikado goes to his local game center to check out what people are playing. "I tried one of >>>>>>>>

"NAMCO ORIGINAL program by EVEZOO." Why'd Endo add his nickname? While making *Xevious*, Endo visited the office of Atari, who would publish the game abroad. Endo recalls, "An Atari staffer asked me: 'What do you do?' I said: 'I write programs, create game content, and make characters.' The staffer replied, 'Oh, you're a game designer. That's what we call a person who does everything at Atari.'" That was when Masanobu Endo decided to start acknowledging himself as a game designer. "Back in '82, there was no understanding about the video-game world. I used the term 'game designer' because I wanted people to think game makers were smart and precise. I'm sure *Pac-Man* creator Toru Iwatani felt the same way." In 1980, Tokyo-based game designer Iwatani created one of the most iconic characters of the twentieth century. The character and the game were a smash, and their success is still felt today. Iwatani received no bonus or salary increase. He was simply a Namco company worker, doing his job.

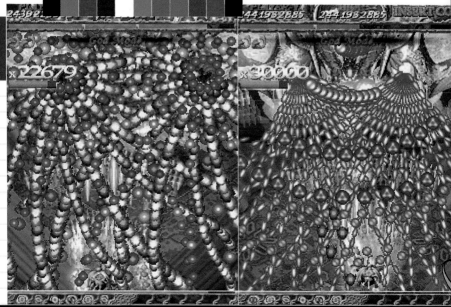

MUSHIHIME-SAMA FUTARI

MUSHIHIME-SAMA CAN FEATURE
TWO THOUSAND BULLETS . . .
ON A SINGLE SCREEN

▷▷▷▷▷▷▷ those maniac shooters," he says. "It was so difficult that I couldn't even clear the first stage. It wasn't fun. I watched a few hard-core players beat stage after stage. There was something exhilarating in watching that." This coming from the man who created the first arcade shooter. "It's a shame that today's shooting games are so hard that most people can't play them."

Shmup specialty developer Cave churns out some of the most challenging games in the genre. "I'd have to say our games are difficult for casual players," says Cave's Tsuneki Ikeda. He's not joking. The hardest setting on Cave shooters such as *Mushihime-sama*, *Pink Sweets*, and *Muchi Muchi Pork* can feature more than two thousand bullets. That's not in the entire game but on a single screen at one time! With its 1995 shmup *DonPachi*, Cave invented the maniac bullet shooter. It's no accident that Cave, which stands for Computer Art Visual Entertainment, focuses predominantly on shmups. "We used to make a bunch

LEFT: RECO FROM *MUSHIHIME-SAMA FUTARI*

of different kinds of games here at Cave," says Ikeda. "But shooters were the ones that sold the best, so that's why we chose to specialize." Before cofounding Cave in 1994, he worked at another shmup specialty developer, Toaplan, which made a series of proto–bullet-hell shooters in the early 1990s. Ikeda showed a knack for weaving complex and beautiful bullet patterns that were challenging like a maze. He didn't set out to be a programmer, but thought being a programmer was the only way to become a game maker. And those programming skills he picked up in a business school of all places. "Back then, there were no schools where you could study game programming," Ikeda explains. >>>>>>>>

"The only place you could study computer programming was in business school. My parents were really surprised when I told them I didn't want to be a salaryman, I wanted to make video games."

After entering Toaplan straight out of school, he was immediately assigned to make a shooter. The game, *Batsugun* (1993), was a Japanese arcade hit. That game set the tone for pretty much every shooter to follow. Unlike other shmups of the time that had long, drawn-out levels that players had to memorize, *Batsugun* featured short levels packed with brightly colored bullet patterns that players committed to memory. Toaplan requested more and more shooting games. But when the developer's

CAVE'S TSUNEKI IKEDA

business went south, Ikeda and his colleagues jumped ship and founded Cave.

At the newly conceived Cave Co., Ltd., the former Toaplan employees wanted to pay tribute to the company where they got their start.

CAVE'S SHOOTERS ARE OFFBEAT

"With *DonPachi*, we wanted to make a Toaplan-esque game, but what was a Toaplan-esque game? I didn't really know. I'd only been at Toaplan for two or three years. *DonPachi* was us trying to make a Toaplan-like game." There was even an in-game hidden message that read "Toaplan Forever." The game's title, *DonPachi*, is a pun: the literal meaning of the Japanese characters in the

MUSHIHIME-SAMA FUTARI ARTWORK

CUTE 'EM UPS

It's bullet hell meets boob hell. Called "cute 'em ups," these shoot 'em ups are drenched in saccharine and sexual innuendo. The subgenre got its start back with Konami's *Parodius* shmup franchise in 1988. The game was a parody of Konami's popular side-scrolling shooter *Gradius*. Subsequent versions of the series got sillier and racier: by the second game, *Parodius Da!* (1990), players were blasting girls in bunny costumes out of bubbles, and there was even a large blonde woman who moaned in pleasure while being sprayed with lasers! Konami's cute 2008 2-D shooter *Otomedius* uses a touchscreen that allows players to let out bombing patterns and jiggle the female character's jiggles. Maniac-shooter specialty developer Cave turned up the cute for its sugary shooting game *PinkSweets ~*

MUCHI MUCHI PORK

Ibara Sorekara ~ (2006) and even more so for *Muchi Muchi Pork* (2007), which features a cast of plump, buxom girls flying around on bikes, unloading bullets. The speed at which players can make the three characters move is actually dependent on their bust size!

MUCHI MUCHI PORK

title is "boss bee," a reference to the game's huge final boss, and is also the onomatopoeia for the sound of shooting guns. The game's plot was downright goofy: players were asked to fight their own former comrades to become the most elite fighter pilot. A "warning" message for enemy bosses that flashed on screen read: THIS IS NOT SIMILATION. GET READY TO DESTOROY THE ENEMY. TARGET FOR THE WEAK POINTS OF F**KIN' MACHINE. DO YOUR BEST YOU HAVE EVER DONE. "I get really embarrassed when I see my old games," Ikeda says with a laugh. The game was pure pixelated adrenaline, and diehard shooter fans demanded more. Several sequels followed.

The shooters from Cave are different, offbeat even. They don't rely on the typical spaceship-in-space convention. In fact, Cave's shooters chucked those conventions out the window. As in *DonPachi*, bug motifs pop up in *Mushihime-sama* and its sequel. The five-level game is set in an insect-ruled future. Players are a bug princess, flying through the forest on a golden beetle and shooting bad insects like scorpions and moths. Another Cave shooter, *Esprade* (1998), features manga-style characters (the high-school stud, the Russian psychic assassin, and the young schoolgirl) with extra sensory perception and special powers that let them fly over futuristic Tokyo. The sequel, *Espgaluda* (2003), even lets players change the sex of their character during play, a move that causes intense bullet patterns to slow down. The game's title refers to the supernatural Hindu and Buddhist mythic birdlike creature, Garuda. Shmup *Guwange* (1999) also visits traditional culture. The game is set in Japan's Muromachi period (1336–1573) and has players shoot up kabuki demons as they pass through settings such as a picturesque village or a snow-covered moun-

ESPGALUDA: SESERI

tain. The company continues to release new arcade shooters every year. >>>

"The fact that Cave is dedicated to making arcade shooters and continues to be successful at doing that is amazing," points out Kenta Cho.

"The genre is going through another golden age," says Minoru Ikeda, founder of INH Co., Ltd., a maker of "superplay" DVDs that feature the country's top arcade players tearing their way through insanely difficult games at the highest difficulty levels—and not just doing it without losing a life, but doing it perfectly. Ikeda knows good games and good gameplay when he sees it. "Developers are releasing innovative and original shmups every year. It's enough to make you go cross-eyed!" Ikeda doesn't look like your stereotypical businessman: he's decked out in a dragon-embroidered jacket, and a colorful scarf is wrapped around his neck. He's playing through an arcade shooting skills test that rates players shmup abilities much like Nintendo's *Brain Age* rates gray-matter power.

Aspiring players watch INH DVDs to marvel and hopefully pick up a few tricks of the trade.

INH'S MINORU IKEDA

While the games pretty much only show the gameplay, the discs have an audio track with player commentary that provides insight into how the superplayers approach gaming. The discs have catchy names like *The Flash Desire Raiden III* or *The Madness Battle Garegga* and come packaged with full-color booklets that are chock-full of conceptual art, tips, and interviews with players. INH actually stands for "Insanity Naked Hunter,"

THE SHOOTING LOVE

シューティングラブ。

Shooting Love Koushien is a shooter tournament named after Koushien Stadium, the home of Osaka baseball team the Hanshin Tigers. The tournament is held at the Club Sega arcade in Tokyo's Shinjuku, where players from around the country gather not just to outshoot each other in *The Shooting Love* but to out-psyche each other. One player, known as the "Mysterious Man," showed up in a Spider-Man costume. Another, called "Tonechi," had three contraptions called Ore Commanders, consisting of "cyborg peripherals," strapped to his arm (see diagram on page 87). Tonechi's rationale for using these mechanical aids was so he could fire missiles nonstop. (There are gaps between the missiles when fired by human hands alone.) And how did Tonechi fare at the 2008 tourney? He came in third place, but got one of his Ore Commanders autographed by one of the developers responsible for *The Shooting Love*.

THE MYSTERIOUS MAN

TONECHI AND HIS ORE COMMANDERS

>>>>>>>> which sounds more like a company that makes adult videos than arcade superplay flicks. The insanity is easy to see, but the naked and the hunter? Ikeda explains: "There used to be three employees, and the letters *I*, *N*, and *H* were the initials of our surnames. But N and H left, and then there was only I." Left scrambling, Ikeda came up with the name Insanity Naked Hunter. Meaningless, but memorable.

Ikeda shoots enormous asteroids, causing them to explode. Dodging debris, he taps the joystick, hitting his wedding ring. "It was difficult to get the first DVDs made. I didn't have connections or money, so I just dove in," says the thirty-three-year-old, who once worked as a game-center manager. He had two goals for the DVDs: promote the game and promote the players. "I wanted to increase chatter about the games and help give new life to game centers," he explains. "We wanted to show how superplayers played the game, provide them with a forum to become better known, and get younger players interested in arcade gaming." Ikeda's shmup skills test results flash on the monitor: his level is listed as "exceedingly high." Companies could see that Ikeda was earnest in his love for

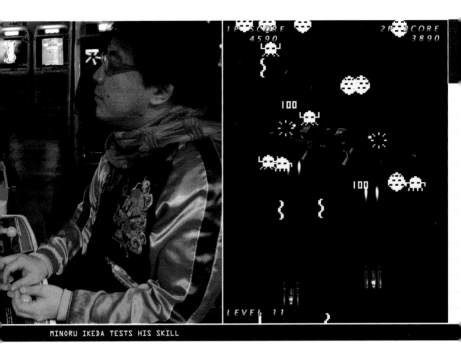

MINORU IKEDA TESTS HIS SKILL

arcade gaming, and he was able to secure deals with major Japanese publishers like Cave and Capcom to produce superplay DVDs with the country's best players. His goods are available in Akihabara retailers and even fill a cabinet at Shinjuku arcade Mikado, where they're up for purchase. After his difficult beginning, he is proud of the company's progress. It hasn't been easy. "It's a miracle we've released so many DVDs," he says. >>>>>>>>

SELF HELP

The Ore Commander is made by famed Japanese peripheral maker Hori. (*Ore* is the masculine form of "I" in Japanese.) Here's how it works: first a battery pack is mounted to the wrist, then the pack is connected to a small motor that is worn on the finger. Once slightly flexed, the finger begins vibrating thirty times a second.

Return to Hey, where Cho presses on. Enemy drones attack from the top and bottom. Cho flips his ship from black to white and back again, absorbing the dark bullets. Each absorbed shot charges up his ship's bombs. "*Ikaruga* has a very innovative game system and a very intuitive interface," he explains. As enemies close in, a giant satellite orb sprays black and white bullets at Cho's spacecraft like a water sprinkler. He bobs and weaves, munching bullets and unleashing chain attacks on enemy craft. The music swells as Cho reaches the stage's boss and shoots at the core, its weak point. The boss goes up in a ball of flames. Light flickers on his glasses. Heading back to Akihabara Station, he passes row after row of retailers selling Wii, PlayStation 3, and Xbox 360 games. "Traditional arcade games are endangered, mainly because of the performance advances of consoles," he says. "But arcade shmups still have deep-rooted popularity. I hope places like Akihabara Hey last a long time." Cho isn't alone. ✿

CLOVER

"Scorer" is Japanese gamer slang for top shmup players. Few scorers get any better than Clover-TAC and Clover-YMN. Both form the duo Clover, a pair of superplayers whose dazzling skills have been featured on superplay DVDs from INH and Konami and even the PlayStation 2 release of Cave shooters *Dodonpachi Dai-Ou-Jou* and *Espgaluda*. The moniker "Clover" not only refers to the lucky-leafed plant, but is also a play on words: "Clover" refers to "CAVE lover," as both TAC and YMN are diehard fans of Cave's bullet-hell shooters. How good are these guys? "I'm pretty proud about scoring 1.04 billion in *Mushihime-sama Futari* on "maniac mode," says TAC. That's more than double the typical high score for finishing the game! But getting that good didn't come cheap. TAC plays six days a week, spending between 3,000 and 5,000 yen each time, while YMN shells out around 2,000 yen a session. TAC sums up the genre's appeal nicely: "With role-playing games, the in-game character's skill level is raised. But with shoot 'em ups, your own skill level is raised."

THE ENIGMATIC CLOVER-YMN (LEFT) AND CLOVER-TAC (RIGHT)

CHO REACHES
THE STAGE'S
BOSS AND
SHOOTS AT
THE CORE,
ITS WEAK
POINT

×4

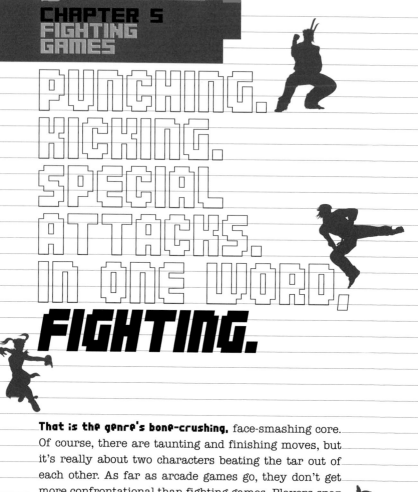

PUNCHING. KICKING. SPECIAL ATTACKS. IN ONE WORD, FIGHTING.

That is the genre's bone-crushing, face-smashing core. Of course, there are taunting and finishing moves, but it's really about two characters beating the tar out of each other. As far as arcade games go, they don't get more confrontational than fighting games. Players spar off with the computer, but at any moment, any random arcade player can hijack that game by inserting a coin and challenging an opponent to a 2-D or 3-D brawl. It's totally anonymous though, as the cabinets in Japan's game centers are placed back-to-back so that players can't see the competition. (Japanese arcade manners dictate that it's rude to even look over the cabinet to check out whom you are playing.) Only the pounding

VIRTUA FIGHTER 5

STREET FIGHTER IV

of buttons or fists on the other side of the cabinet provides any indication of a human opponent. After winning or losing, the challenger can slip away, unnoticed by his or her foe, into the smoky game-center crowds.

It wasn't always that way. The earliest *Street Fighter II* cabinets that came out in 1991 were like the machines found in Europe and North America: the one-player and two-player controls were side by side. There was something peacefully tranquil—Zen, even—about those original cabi-

nets. The machines featured two coin slots: one for hundred-yen coins and the other for fifty-yen coins. A hundred yen would buy two players one head-to-head match, meaning that two friends could sit down and have one game of *Street Fighter II*. After the match, the game was over for both players, leaving neither with hard feelings. It was possible to challenge other players, but it was less of a challenge and more of an intrusion. There was the matter of walking up to the machine while another player was

STREET FIGHTER ZERO 2 CABINET

playing, putting in a coin that altered the game from single-player to two-player, and then standing next to this unknown opponent while duking it out with him or her. Incredibly intimidating if the player was great!

THE GAME NEEDED SOMETHING TO MAXIMIZE ITS TWO-PLAYER POSSIBILITIES

LINKED GAME CABINETS   THE MIKADO GAME CENTER IN SHINJUKU

Yet *Street Fighter II* wasn't hitting its full coin-box potential. It was a two-player game, but was typically played by just one player. The game needed something to maximize its two-player possibilities—and encourage Japanese players to beat up random strangers. An unnamed arcade owner hit upon a clever solution: modify two cabinets so that they were connected to the same motherboard and then put those cabinets back-to-back. That way, expert players could continue playing on one coin, while lousy players kept feeding the machine in hopes of victory and were given a degree of privacy should they lose. This loser-pays model proved so successful that it was adapted not just by *Street Fighter II* developer Capcom, but by the entire Japanese gaming industry. The peaceful two-player one-off-match mode was dropped in Japan altogether.

No one steps up to challenge superplayer Daigo Umehara. He's breezing through 2-D fighter *Super Street Fighter II X: Grand Master Challenge* in Shinjuku game center Mikado. *Street Fighter* character Ryu socks a *shoryuken* "rising dragon fist" into a green savage called Blanka, sending him flat on his back. Ryu unleashes a hurricane kick, but Blanka's up on his feet, charging. Umehara moves the >>>>>>>>>

DAIGO UMEHARA, ARCADE FIGHTER. BLANKA, STREET FIGHTER.

© CAPCOM U.S.A., INC.

UMEHARA PRESSES THE PUNCH BUTTON, WHICH PLANTS A HADOKEN IN BLANKA'S FACE

last time I was in one before today." Umehara has quit, cold turkey.
The game was sucking up too much of his time, energy, and money.
At twenty-six years old, he's already retired.

Street Fighter II wasn't the first fighter (heck, it wasn't the first
Street Fighter), but it had the biggest impact of any fighting game.
Sega introduced the first arcade fisticuffs in Japan way back in
1976. Called *Heavyweight Champ*, it was a black-and-white punch
'em up where the controls were inside a pair of plastic boxing
gloves attached to the cabinet, for real-time in-game punching.

║║║ ║║║║║
PLAYER 4

DAIGO UMEHARA rose to fame as one of the best 2-D fighting players in the world: two-times winner of both the Tougeki-Super Battle Opera, an annual fighting tournament hosted by Japanese arcade magazine *Arcadia*, and America's oldest and most prestigious fighting tourney, the EVO Championship Series. Umehara set his sights on mastering *Street Fighter* when he was in his early teens. From the age of fourteen to eighteen, the now twenty-six-year-old Umehara played *Street Fighter II* seven hours a day on average. Every day. He spent Y80,000 a month on feeding the game with coins. Umehara recalls, "I saved and scrimped, worked odd jobs, and used my lunch money so I could play." He studied up, buying play guides that explained each character's moves, watched others, and played like hell. Umehara seems like the kind of guy you'd want to pick your horses at the Tokyo Derby—not because he's lucky, but rather because he'd research down to how humidity affected the dirt track. By the time he was in his late teens, Umehara wasn't good, he was great, regularly

placing at big tournaments. Sure, there were monetary prizes, but you can't live on a few thousand bucks once or twice a year. Umehara was playing simply because he wanted to be able to walk into any arcade and whip anyone's ass. At the same time, Umehara has reached a point where there are only a handful of players on this earth who are challenging for him to take on. "It's not that it's boring to play regular players," Umehara says, "It's just more interesting to play against really great players." There's a purity in that.

A couple more fighting games appeared in the mid-1980s: *Karate Champ* (1984), from Technos, with dual joysticks for two-player battles and *Yie Ar Kung-Fu* (1985), from Konami, which added weapons such as ninja stars to the mix of punching and kicking. The genre never quite took off though, as Japanese game centers were still dominated by shooting games. "The first fighting game I played was *Karate Champ*," recalls Sega's *Virtua Fighter 5* game director Daichi Katagiri. "I was only a little kid then, and I didn't have that much money to play it." The 8-bit *Karate Champ* didn't

feature health bars that showed the player's energy level, but put emphasis on who could land the most blows within the allotted time. In the late 1980s, Capcom released the first *Street Fighter*, which originally put more emphasis on beating up the arcade cabinet than opponents. The cabinet was outfitted with three pressure-sensitive pads that measured how hard players hit them to dish out attacks

EARLY FIGHTING GAME *KARATE CHAMP*

that varied between light, medium, and hard. These were eventually abandoned after continual damage to the cabinets (and player injuries) in favor of the current six-button layout. "When I was in junior high school, I remember seeing *Street Fighter* in the arcades, but I didn't play it because I was more into shooting games," says Hideaki Itsuno, one of Capcom's game developers. Ironic, as Itsuno would later go on to head up Capcom's reworking of the original *Street Fighter* with *Street Fighter Zero* (1995).

Shooters were still king of the game centers in the late 1980s. They had become heavily based on memory, however. Players spent more time watching other players play (and die) in hopes of memorizing elaborate levels and not wasting their own coins. But in 1991, *Street Fighter II* brought back an enjoyable game experience. It was fresh! As with early shooting games, it inspired the if-I'm-good-I-can-keep-playing feeling. "I remember all my friends started playing *Street Fighter II*," says Umehara. "It was really fun to play against each other, and to see who was best." Osaka-based Capcom had a megahit on its hands. The game

SLIT-SKIRTED CHUN-LI WAS ARGUABLY ONE OF GAMING'S FIRST STRONG FEMALE ACTION HEROINES

STREET FIGHTER II AND CHUN-LI

CAPCOM'S HIDEAKI ITSUNO

captured the public's imagination, and the sequel spawned an anime, a Hollywood movie with Jean-Claude Van Damme and Kylie Minogue, and a Hong Kong action-movie spoof in which Jackie Chan dressed up as slit-skirted Chun-Li, a character that was arguably one of gaming's first strong female action heroines. According to *Donkey Kong* and *Mario* creator Shigeru Miyamoto, Nintendo designed the Super Famicom home console controller with six buttons just so the company could release *Street Fighter II* in homes. As for most of the players of Umehara's generation, *Street Fighter II* was the game to play. And for Japanese game developers, it was the game to beat.

>>>>>>>>>

STREET FIGHTER IV CHARACTERS

>>>>>>>> **The early 1990s saw another fighter** from another Osaka-based developer: SNK (now known as SNK Playmore) released *Fatal Fury: The King of Fighters*, a game that immediately gave SNK its own niche in the genre with its stylish characters and its exceedingly powerful arcade hardware. SNK even created a home version of its arcade hardware with the astronomically priced Neo-Geo Advanced Entertainment System, which retailed at US $599. Most balked at the insanely high price tag, but according to SNK, the home console was popular among Middle Eastern princes. The SNK arcade cabinets

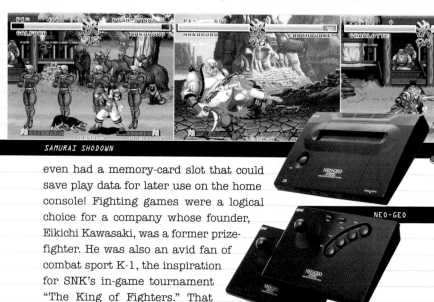

SAMURAI SHODOWN

NEO-GEO

even had a memory-card slot that could save play data for later use on the home console! Fighting games were a logical choice for a company whose founder, Eikichi Kawasaki, was a former prize-fighter. He was also an avid fan of combat sport K-1, the inspiration for SNK's in-game tournament "The King of Fighters." That tourney started in SNK game *Fatal Fury* and was later spun off into its own series, *The King of Fighters*. Company boss Kawasaki was known to interrupt programmers to physically demonstrate exactly how a punch was thrown or how characters should take blows. Staffers hit the nearby game centers to soak up the vibe and check out what players were into. The bruisers that SNK churned out were steeped in Kawasaki's street smarts and the grime of Osaka. The games were hits.

SNK brought new twists to the 2-D fighting game. Its four-button layout economically used the Start button in-game for taunting and insulting opponents. In *Art of Fighting* (1992), SNK introduced a rechargeable "spirit meter" that was separate from a character's health bar and allowed fighters to perform special moves. What's more, a "camera zoom" was introduced that zoomed in when the opponents were close together but pulled back when they were far apart. Its *King of Fighters '94* would create a fresh three-on-three fighting

THE KING OF FIGHTERS '94

KAWASAKI WAS KNOWN TO INTERRUPT PROGRAMMERS TO PHYSICALLY DEMONSTRATE EXACTLY HOW A PUNCH WAS THROWN

system that had trios go one-on-one with each other. These teams of three fighters would face off until the last fighter had lost. This fighting system would show up as an optional mode in fighting games *Tekken* (1994) from Namco (now known as NBGI) and *Dead or Alive* (1996) from Tecmo. SNK's 1993 title, *Samurai Shodown* (known as *Samurai Spirits* in Japan), was the first to introduce weapon-based fighting, a subgenre that would lead to popular titles like Arc System Works' *Guilty Gear* (1998) and Namco's *Soulcalibur* (1998). But with SNK titles, it was all about fist to face. "Punching is important," says SNK producer Shinya Kimoto. "When you hit a button, a direct response is important. That, and the sound effects of smacking someone."

New characters trickled out a few at a time with each iteration of *Street Fighter*, but flooded out of the SNK fighting games. ⟩⟩⟩⟩⟩⟩⟩⟩⟩

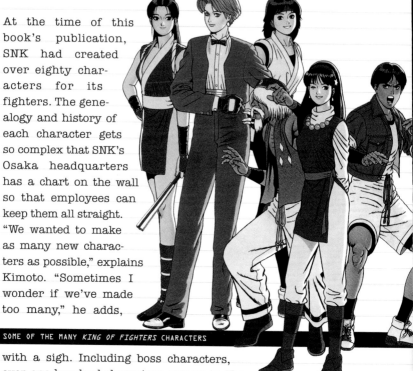

At the time of this book's publication, SNK had created over eighty characters for its fighters. The genealogy and history of each character gets so complex that SNK's Osaka headquarters has a chart on the wall so that employees can keep them all straight. "We wanted to make as many new characters as possible," explains Kimoto. "Sometimes I wonder if we've made too many," he adds,

SOME OF THE MANY *KING OF FIGHTERS* CHARACTERS

with a sigh. Including boss characters, over one hundred characters appear in *The King of Fighters* series alone! While other developers judiciously release a few new characters at carefully spaced intervals, SNK often seems like it's just throwing spaghetti at the wall and seeing what sticks. Perhaps, but SNK's characters are so cool looking and so stylish! They seem taller than characters in other games, with bod-

OVER ONE HUNDRED CHARACTERS APPEAR IN THE KING OF FIGHTERS

ies eight or nine heads high. They also ooze personality: from a white-haired female Mexican wrestler to a tornado-spinning Catholic priest out to redeem foes; from a junior high school Russian-Japanese girl with expert sumo abilities to cloned brawlers out to get the fighter they were cloned from. For SNK, as long as the character is badass, the company runs with it. Capcom is more judicious, introducing a few new characters at a time.

THE KING OF FIGHTERS XII

With fewer characters in *Street Fighter*, however, each one somehow seems to count more—as if they are chess pieces with certain strengths and abilities unique to that character alone.

It was *Street Fighter* that captivated Daigo Umehara and catapulted him to fame as one of the best fighting players in the world. Now he's so good, he's run out of challengers. "I used to wish there was a pro level," Umehara says, landing a kick into Bruce Lee-like character Fei Long. "But I don't really care much about that anymore." He unleashes another combo. "I don't want to be half-assed," he says. "I'm either going to play or not play. Right now, I'm not playing at all." Umehara's not even looking at the

"FOR THOSE OF US INVOLVED IN CREATING THE STREET FIGHTER GAMES, PLAYERS LIKE DAIGO ARE TRULY WONDERFUL"

"THE BEAST" VS. JUSTIN WONG

It's the *Street Fighter* match everyone talks about. New York player Justin Wong duked it out with Tokyo's Daigo Umehara, who's known in the West as just Daigo or "The Beast" for his aggressive fighting style. Immortalized by YouTube, the now infamous 2004 match at the EVO Championship Series fighting tournament didn't take place in the neon glare of a Japanese game center, but under the leafy palm trees of California State Polytechnic University. Umehara and Wong sat side by side in front of a CRT television and went head to head in *Street Fighter III: 3rd Strike* with Umehara, playing as fighter Ken, taking Wong, playing as Chun-Li. The match was projected on a big screen in an auditorium packed with spectators. The first match was all Umehara, but Wong came back and defeated him in the second match. It all came down to the third, tiebreaking match. Wong got

THE REVOLUTIONARY *VIRTUA FIGHTER*

flickering screen. "For those of us involved in creating the *Street Fighter* games, players like Daigo are truly wonderful," says Capcom's Hideaki Itsuno. "This isn't something like PC gaming in Korea where you can land a pro contract and play professionally, but rather just playing because you want to truly understand a game. Then again, I have no idea where he got his money." What does Umehara have to show for the thousands of dollars he sunk in Tokyo arcades? Apart from being really good at *Street Fighter* . . . nothing.

his licks in early, but was defensive, crouching in a turtle style. It worked: Umehara's health bar was drained to a couple of pixels. Wong unleashed a fifteen-hit super combo, but The Beast parried each hit. The crowd got to its feet, cheering Umehara on. He unleashed a counter attack, landing blow after blow, finishing Wong off and sending his character Chun-Li high into the air. Coming back from what looked like certain death, Umehara beat Wong.

"At the time, I didn't think much of it," The Beast recalls. "But when I saw the footage, I was surprised that I was able to pull out that win." Wong was gracious in defeat: "Everyone hopes for a match like that at some stage in their career. I did good but obviously he clutched out for the win. He is the type that will figure out your style of play within the space of one game. I was very happy to play him. It's something I'll never forget."

>>>>>>>> **While 2-D _Street Fighter II_ was ruling the game centers,** Sega brought another dimension to fighters. Literally. When it was first released in 1993, Sega's _Virtua Fighter_ was revolutionary: it was in 3-D. Designed by Sega's resident genius Yu Suzuki in the company's Amusement Machine Research and Development Department 2, _Virtua Fighter_ featured fully polygonal characters. The game ran on an arcade system board that Sega codeveloped with the aerospace company that eventually became Lockheed Martin. Compared to _Street Fighter II_'s six-button layout, the _Virtua Fighter_ three-button Punch-Kick-Guard layout seemed streamlined—simple even. It was anything but. Even though the game was a technological marvel for its time, many were put off by the tournament-style rules whereby players could lose just by getting knocked out of bounds. The following year saw another _Virtua Fighter_ with improved graphics and fighting. Each installment in

CHARACTERS FROM _VIRTUA FIGHTER 5_

the series produced more realistic 3-D graphics and inspired other three-dimensional fighters like _Tekken_ and _Dead or Alive_. It was akin to the change from black-and-white to color TV. Two-dimensional pixelized fighting games were suddenly "dated" and "old fashioned." 3-D fighting games became so popular that 2-D fighter stalwart SNK released a 3-D spin-off brawler called _The King of Fighters: Maximum Impact_ in 2004. The game lacked that classic SNK feel. But _The King of Fighters XII_ (2008) is a return to form. During development, the characters were rendered in 3-D but then converted to 2-D. The game is 2.5-D! SNK is porting it from arcades to the PlayStation 3, the Xbox 360, and the PC. This is SNK's new business model: create arcade games and then port them to every platform.

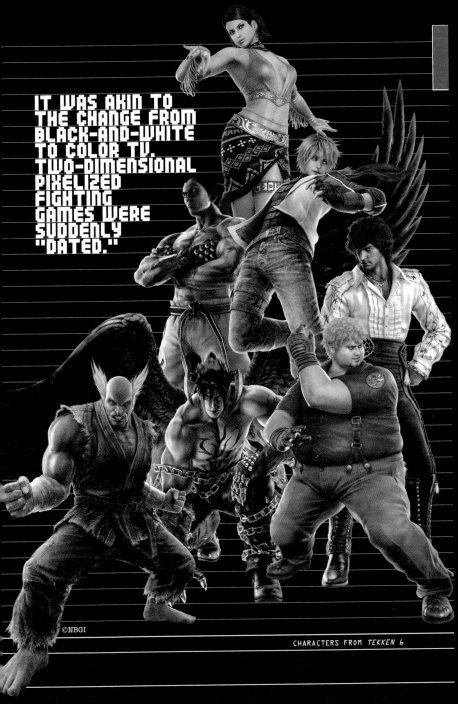

IT WAS AKIN TO
THE CHANGE FROM
BLACK-AND-WHITE
TO COLOR TV.
TWO-DIMENSIONAL
PIXELIZED
FIGHTING
GAMES WERE
SUDDENLY
"DATED."

©NBGI

CHARACTERS FROM *TEKKEN 6*

"We have to release our fighting games in arcades," says SNK exec Soichiro Hosoya. "If we didn't, nobody would buy the console games."

The *Virtua Fighter* games put strong emphasis on a series of very calculated moves heavily based on timing. All of the characters are balanced such that no one particular character is "better" than

"THERE'S SOMETHING ABOUT SQUARING OFF AGAINST SOMEONE IN THE SAME SPACE AND TIME"

AKIHABARA CLUB SEGA HAD 43 *VF5* CABINETS   DAICHI KATAGIRI

another. Since timing is vital, the meticulous *Virtua Fighter* team didn't add online to the PlayStation 3 port of *Virtua Fighter 5* because it was worried that possible online delays might mean a millisecond advantage or disadvantage for players. In an age where online is de rigueur for console games, *VF5* on the PS3 was still a hit in Japan. "There are customers who bought the console version just to practice," says Sega's *Virtua Fighter 5* game director Daichi Katagiri, who's been with the series since the start. After getting good in the privacy of their own homes, players then show up in arcades to publicly pummel other players. That's not to say the *Virtua Fighter* arcade team are game-center purists who thumb their collective nose at connected console gaming. "Both online play and arcade play have their merits," says Katagiri. "With online play, you can enjoy taking on others in the comfort of your own home. But, for arcade play, there's something about squaring off against someone in the same space and time." When the game was originally released, Sega rolled out forty-three *Virtua Fighter 5* cabinets at its Akihabara Club Sega in Tokyo. Only one of those was dedicated to single play.

Virtua Fighter 5 runs on a powerful state-of-the-art arcade system board called the Sega Lindbergh. But power isn't everything for fighters. Take *Melty Blood: Act Cadenza*, made in 2005 by French-Bread, a *doujin* (fan-created) developer. It runs on the Sega NAOMI computer board, the arcade version of the system that powered the Sega

VF5'S PAI CHAN

Dreamcast console—in 1999. Even though *Melty Blood: Act Cadenza* plays like a standard fighter, it is anything but typical. The doujin 2-D fighter is based on another doujin game called *Tsukihime* (2000) from amateur developer Type-Moon and was originally designed and programmed for home PCs back in 2002. *Tsukihime* follows a young, pocket-knife wielding boy who is able to see "death lines" on people. "The story and the characters are really interesting," says Nobuya Narita of French-Bread (a name that came about because one of its developers really likes French bread). "We thought that the story had many combat elements and was suitable for a fighting game." In short: *Melty Blood* is an amateur game based on another amateur game.

>>>>>>>>>

MELTY BLOOD

Narita and a friend first started making PC games for fun back in the late nineties, whenever they hung out. They specialize in amateur punch 'em ups. "Fighting games are easy to make," Narita points out. "Other genres, like shooting or action, are a pain in the ass. Lazy, I know . . ." The original *Melty Blood* for PC was an indie hit. The game has a certain appeal that sets it apart, and is charming even to those unfamiliar with the *Tsukihime* source material. Characters such as a robotic maid or a maid with a

"WE USED TO DO WHATEVER WE WANTED, BUT NOW WE HAVE TO TAKE INTO ACCOUNT WHAT THE PLAYERS WANT"

special spatula attack are less "cool" and more otaku-flavored than other fighting games with muscle-bound brawlers. Type-Moon gave its blessing, and *Melty Blood* ended up in arcades in spring 2005 and on the PS2 the following year. French-Bread officially went pro.

"Turning pro isn't so rare these days," explains Narita. He's right: more and more doujin software groups (called "doujin circles" in Japan) are becoming professional developers. Doujin software is not a new phenomenon in Japan and has existed in varying degrees as long as there's been personal computers. The doujin game scene really exploded with the advent of Windows, however, which streamlined and simplified the game development process for amateurs. "Doujin is really hard to define," says Narita.

GUILTY GEAR

DESTROYED

Guilty Gear is here not to just punch your teeth in, but also to rock your face off. While other fighting games look to Hong Kong martial-arts films for inspiration, *Guilty Gear* looks to glam rock and heavy metal. "My favorite band hands down is Queen," says Daisuke Ishiwatari, the game's creator. "I also really like Judas Priest and Mötley Crüe." The South Africa-born Ishiwatari first got interested in creating fighting games while at vocational school in mid-1990s Japan. "I wanted to design characters, tell a story, create something interactive, and make music," recalls Ishiwatari. "For me, fighting games were the complete package." He got his start in the industry working at SNK, getting his chops on historical fighter *The Last Blade* (1997), before going to work at Tokyo developer Arc System Works and creating rock-and-roll fighter *Guilty Gear* (1998). The lurid game takes place during a fighting tournament in a dreary twenty-second-century society that has been torn apart by war against brutal bio-organisms called Gears. Besides designing the characters, penning the story, and making the game's metal soundtrack, Ishiwatari also voiced main character Sol Badguy—a character whose favorite album is Queen's "Sheer Heart Attack" and whose real name is Freddie. That's no coincidence as Queen lead singer Freddie Mercury's nickname was Mr. Bad Guy! The game bangs out rocker reference after rocker reference: characters have special moves named after Metallica songs and the theme music is reminiscent of Led Zeppelin. "I love the sound of heavy guitar distortion," says Ishiwatari. "And when the lyrics kick in, I just want to scream along. It's one of those things that keeps me going." Rock on, Ishiwatari, rock on.

STREET FIGHTER IV

>>>>>>>> "It's about people making games they want to make in their free time." These amateur developers do hope to sell their work, typically at events like Japan's twice-annual doujin convention Comiket. "If doujin circles sell their games, all the better," he says. "That way they can make more games." But there are growing pains in going from doujin hobbyist to doujin corporate. "It's changed for us," says Narita. "We used to do whatever we wanted, but now we have to take into account what the players want."

Porting doujin computer game *Melty Blood* to arcades was atypical. Running on dated hardware, it was still an arcade smash, securing a coveted slot in the Tougeki-Super Battle Opera fighting tournament, producing a PlayStation 2 port, a serialized manga, and a sequel called *Melty Blood: Actress Again* (2008). The arcade port of the home-console version also got a PC port. "When we were making *Melty Blood*, we thought that it might be popular because *Tsukihime* was so popular," says Narita. "But we had no idea it would be this popular for this long." Not bad for a 2-D fighter running on old hardware! With heavy pixels, so-so music and sparse backgrounds, the game lacks the polish of fighters made by SNK and Capcom. The game's low-tech elements didn't push away arcade players, however. It endeared them. The success of this amateur game actually forced

STREET FIGHTER IV

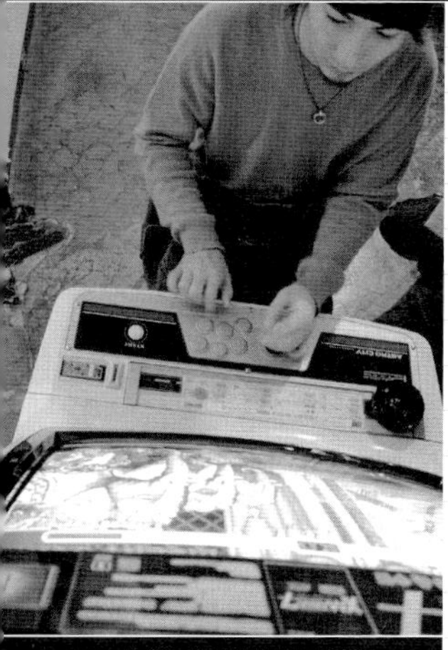

"THE BEAST" AT WORK

IN LESS THAN FIFTEEN MINUTES, DAIGO UMEHARA CLEARS STREET FIGHTER II, AND HE DID IT ON ONE COIN

big companies like Capcom to reassess their arcade business. "Because an inexpensive fighter like *Melty Blood* has become a big hit," says Capcom's Itsuno, "I've been telling my bosses that perhaps we should take another look at how we do arcade fighters."

In less than fifteen minutes, Daigo Umehara clears *Street Fighter II*, and he did it on one coin. Umehara isn't impressed, saying, "Anyone can do that these days" and, "It's no big deal." He gets up from the green velvet seat and pushes it in under the cabinet. How was it playing *Street Fighter II* again? He chuckles. "If I do return," Umehara says, "you can bet I'll be playing a full seven hours a day." With the advent of *Street Fighter IV*, smart money says Umehara will come back fighting.

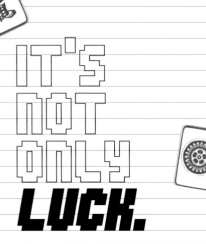

CHAPTER 6
GAMES OF
CHANCE

IT'S
NOT
ONLY
LUCK.

This is gaming where the odds matter as much as skill. Maybe more, even. Whether it's electronic mahjong or arcade pachinko, this isn't gambling. There isn't money to be won legally, and the stakes aren't higher than other arcade games. But don't tell that to the players.

The mahjong-game section of the Namco Wonder Tower arcade is hopping. On the sixth floor, over-looking the heart of elegant Kyoto where geisha and fashionista foot traffic mingle, couples, businessmen, and dudes in T-shirts huddle around a long, glowing *Sega Network Taisen Mahjong MJ4* cabinet. Burning bright with green lights, the cabinet is divided up into individual touchscreens and benches. Haruka Sakurai sashays through the arcade in a denim miniskirt, looking for an open place to sit and grab a game of

SEGA NETWORK TAISEN MAHJONG MJ4

virtual mahjong. "Arcade mahjong is getting more and more popular," she says. "It's because of games like *MJ4*." She finds a seat, feeds the machine two hundred yen, gets out her Sega-issued *MJ4* mahjong-pro data card that's given only to pros who appear in-game, and slides it into the card reader. Her name pops up on the screen, along with her picture. "Argh," she says, covering the on-screen avatar photo. "This is so not my favorite picture of myself." Haruka, a professional mahjong player, appears in-game as herself and has since *MJ2*. The game is networked throughout Japan, and Haruka comes here regularly to play a round of mahjong with opponents from anywhere across the country.

THE NEW SHINBASHI BUILDING, TOKYO

Most Japanese arcades, like Namco Wonder Tower, have games of chance. Some have more than others—Shibuya's Sega Gigo has one floor dedicated to medal games and the pinball-like game pachinko, and another floor dedicated to Vegas-style gambling, complete with blackjack dealers. Mahjong has an entire building dedicated to it: the New Shinbashi Building in Tokyo's Shinbashi. From the outside, it looks like just another 1970s architectural tragedy. The white plaster latticework hasn't aged well. On any weekday, you'll see businessmen in ill-fitting suits transiting in and out, and gaggles of young girls wearing thigh-highs and high heels clustered in the building's doorways, putting on eyeliner and talking on cell phones. Typical. Inside, it's anything but.

"A building filled with real mahjong and arcade mahjong?" asks pro player Haruka Sakurai. "That's rather unusual." Unusual, indeed. The ground floor looks nondescript: drug stores, tiny clothing shops, and smoky cafés. But the first three floors of the four-story New Shinbashi Building have about fifteen individual arcades, all dedicated to mahjong. The top floor of the New Shinbashi Building doesn't have game centers, but actual mahjong parlors with green felt tables and plastic tiles that players can handle. Through a crack

in a door, women in plain office-lady type uniforms are glimpsed serving drinks to four men sitting at a table as the hypnotic sound of tiles being shuffled is heard. They're playing mahjong. Real mahjong, for real money. The second floor is an endless row of massage therapists with open doorways revealing green-curtained cubicles. One massage parlor offers way more than massages at hourly rates. A worn woman in a skimpy skirt and unfashionable shoes shuffles down the linoleum hallway, past an ad for an adult movie theater taped to the wall. The building seethes sinister. >>>>>>>>>>

Out front of the arcades, banners advertise Sega's *MJ4*, in which players can challenge each other or virtual in-game mahjong pros, including a virtual version of Haruka. The arcades in this building are all dedicated to mahjong. "It's always been that way," says the orange-shirted arcade employee at one of those arcades. Are they all owned by the same company? "No, they're all separate," he replies. But why all the mahjong arcade games? His reply is simple: "Because it's popular." And he's right. It is.

Mahjong is a complex game with complex rules. There are 144 tiles total, with suits that include bamboo, dots, flowers, Chinese characters, winds, and dragons. After turning the

"IN AMERICA, WHEN YOU MENTION MAHJONG, MOST PEOPLE THINK OF OLDER JEWISH WOMEN GETTING TOGETHER TO NOSH, CHATTER, AND PLAY"

TOM SLOPER

144 tiles face-down and mixing them, each player builds a wall of tiles that are used to create patterns, or rather, hands, of predetermined combinations. Taking turns, players discard the tiles they don't need and select new ones from the remaining tiles. The Japanese version of the game uses an intricate system to categorize points to determine the winner. This intricate scoring system is one of the elements that makes mahjong a logical candidate for an arcade version of the game.

In her late teens, Haruka got a part-time job handing out fliers for a mahjong parlor in Osaka. "I guess I was always interested in mahjong as a game," she says. A quick learner, Haruka studied how the parlor's pros played, and picked up the rules. "The first time I finally did play," Haruka recalls, "I got a *yakuman*, which is the strongest hand of tiles a player can get." On the spot, the owner of the parlor asked her if she wanted to switch from handing out fliers

PLAYER 6

Twenty-seven-year-old tile shark Haruka Sakurai is quick to point out that mahjong isn't gambling, it's a game. "Here in Japan, the perception of mahjong really needs to change," she says. "It hasn't had a great image over the years." But arcade versions are part of the reason for mahjong's increasing respectability. "Of course, the difference between arcade mahjong and actual mahjong is the same as the difference between video-game baseball and real baseball," she says.

But for Japanese players looking to casually play, game centers offer an ideal option, she believes. "I want more adults, more women to play. I want more children to play. I want more people to understand what a great game mahjong is."

to playing mahjong. Haruka accepted and took a spot in the parlor's miniskirt-wearing, all-female "Cherry Blossom" group of players. "I didn't tell my parents about accepting that job," says Haruka. "Mahjong doesn't exactly have a wholesome image in Japan."

Mahjong is very much a cash game in Japan. It's gambling, it's cool, and it's somewhat taboo. These connotations attract male players. "In Japan, the majority of the players are male," says video-game producer Tom Sloper, who worked in Japan and produced the *Shanghai* mahjong series for American game publisher Activision in 1986. "Yes, there are female players and pros in Japan, but it's far from fifty-fifty male to female. But in China, the game is less dominated by male players." For the Chinese, mahjong is a game for friends and family, typically played at home during holidays. In the US, the game is predominantly played by old ladies and has ⟫⟫⟫⟫⟫⟫

been since the National Mah Jongg League was founded in 1937. The league was founded by women to promote an Americanized version of mahjong designed to appeal to women. "In America, when you mention mahjong, most people immediately think of older Jewish women getting together to nosh, chatter, and play," Sloper says. In Japan, men get together to gamble, smoke, and play at mahjong parlors, where they might play for ten thousand yen a hand. (Professional players like Haruka don't put down their own money, but are salaried by the parlors they work for.)

After honing her skills against male customers, Haruka turned pro when she was twenty-four. Turning pro in Japanese mahjong means passing a test that's cleverly called, well, "The Pro Test." The once-a-year national examination consists of a written section, an interview, and a practical hands-on test, in other words, playing.

MAHJONG'S ORIGINS

There are several theories about mahjong's origins. Like most things in China, its creation is attributed to Confucius, who supposedly invented the game back in 500 BC. The name "mahjong," which means "sparrow" in Chinese, comes from Confucius's love of his feathered friends. Sounds nice and all, but the fact that the game doesn't have a recorded historical appearance until the mid-nineteenth century doesn't give that theory much gumption. The most commonly accepted theory is that it was a combination of existing Chinese card and domino games. Modified versions of the ivory-tiled game had found a ready audience in neighboring Japan by the early twentieth century.

"MAHJONG IS 75 PERCENT LUCK AND 25 PERCENT SKILL. IT'S IN THAT LAST 25 PERCENT WHERE THE GAME IS PLAYED."

She passed with flying colors. "After I went pro," says Haruka, "I finally told my parents about my mahjong playing job. Turning pro, I think, helped justify it." Making a living for pro players can consist of competing in cash-prize tournaments with other pros, or working at mahjong parlors. Haruka plays

MAHJONG PRO HARUKA SAKURAI

five times a week and is on the clock for seven hours a day. That doesn't mean she's playing straight through—some days she only plays for an hour or two if the parlor's not busy. "Mahjong is 75 percent luck and 25 percent skill," she says. "It's in that last 25 percent where the game is played." When pros like Haruka lose to amateur players, they say it wasn't skill that beat them, but luck.

Back in 2004, Haruka was one of the players selected to appear in *Sega Network Taisen Mahjong MJ2* as the result of a recommendation from the Japan Professional Mahjong League. Sega's *Network Taisen Mahjong* series boasts a selection of male and female pros, not just as eye candy but as virtual opponents for amateur arcade players. Haruka has been with the arcade franchise ever since *MJ2*. Since mahjong is a four-player game, arcade players can battle it out one of three ways: against three CPU players, against players in the same arcade, or against players in other arcades across Japan. The difference between virtual and real mahjong? "You can't read the other player's vibes," says Haruka.

Mahjong arcade games were a no-brainer. "There's something like ten million mahjong players in Japan," says Sega mahjong >>>>>>>>>

PLAYING THE PONIES, THE ELECTRIC PONIES

STARHORSE2

In **1981,** amusement-game company Sigma (now known as pachinko parlor and arcade company Adores) had an international hit on its hands when it released horse-racing game *The Derby Mark III.* While the series was strictly a medal game in Japan, *The Derby Mark III* was located in Las Vegas gambling casinos, spitting out quarters instead of worthless arcade medals. Sigma's *Derby* series featured electromagnetic mechanical horses racing around a miniature track. Very primitive! By the early 1990s, Sega's *Royal Ascot* (1991) had integrated mechanical horses and a small model horse track with large video monitors that played the race in real time. For those not content with simply betting, Sega's *StarHorse* (2000) puts players in charge of micromanaging the animals too. Players must groom their horses between races by

rubbing the touchscreens, and feed them things like carrots and radishes. It's even possible to give the horses the Japanese equivalent of Red Bull energy drinks. Since players sit at these horse-racing medal games for long periods of time, *StarHorse2* features up to twenty-one individual seats, all with hi-def touchscreens, side tables, and mesh seat backs for extra comfort and support—an elaborate setup that snagged a prestigious Good Design Award from the Japan Industrial Design Promotion Organization. Many arcades even put small trash cans next to individual seats, as players are known to drink countless cans of coffee, chain-smoke, or munch on snacks while playing. Just like at the real racetrack!

STARHORSE2 CABINETS

game planner Katsuhiko Saito. "It's more popular than Japanese chess (*shoji*), Western chess, and the board game Go." However, its image is nowhere near as pristine as chess. "In Japan, if someone says they're a shoji teacher, people are impressed," Haruka says. "If someone says they're a mahjong pro, people think you're a gambler. It's not fair—both games are intellectual." Mahjong games have been an arcade mainstay since solitaire-type mahjong games appeared in the early 1980s. By the

KATSUHIKO SAITO

"THERE'S SOMETHING LIKE TEN MILLION MAHJONG PLAYERS IN JAPAN. IT'S MORE POPULAR THAN JAPANESE CHESS"

late 1980s, graphics had improved and could render game elements such as tiles more realistically. Tiles were not the only things that could be realistically rendered. Game developer Seta, disappointed with the sluggish performance of its 1987 arcade title *Super Real Mahjong PI*, added a sure-fire spin to the sequel: stripping. *Super Real Mahjong PII* featured seventeen-year-old "heroine" Shoko in various states of undress. Arcade-game magazine *Gamest* published images from the game, doubling the game's sales and making it a smash hit. A glut of naughty mahjong games followed, including *Shisen-Sho Joshiryo-Hen* (1989), from Tamtex, which "rewarded" players with naked pixelated beauties. Venerated shmup developer PSiKYO was acquired by game company X-nauts and began focusing on mahjong games with titles such as *Taisen Hot Gimmick 4 Ever* or *G-Taste Mahjong*. Things picked up steam when pixels where traded for actual adult video clips and these over-eighteen mahjong arcade games stopped beating around the bush: this was pornography.

>>>>>>>>

Sex sells, sure, but the suggestive imagery did more than titillate. It took players' minds off the computer AI. "Networked play was but a future dream at that time," says Tom Sloper. Then, in 2002, along came Konami's *Mah-jong Fight Club* and the dream became reality. The game had a network function that meant you could face off against other players in the same arcade. And this new game was classy too. Classy and simple. *Mah-jong Fight Club* wasn't about trying to get some woman to take off her shirt. It was about playing mahjong! While previous mahjong games featured a row of buttons on arcade

IN THE POSTWAR YEARS THERE WAS A CIGARETTE SHORTAGE. BUT WITH PACHINKO, IT WAS POSSIBLE TO WIN TOBACCO.

POSTWAR PACHINKO PARLOR

cabinets, an intimidating sight for new players, *Mah-jong Fight Club* franchise used a touchscreen. Its network function was rapidly enhanced to allow play between real players across Japan. Likewise, Sega introduced its *Network Taisen Mahjong MJ* series in 2002, which let players battle each other and virtual pro players. While Sega had been making realistic arcade mahjong games since the mid-1990s with titles like *Pro Mahjong ExtremeS* and *Virtual Mahjong*, those games were lost in the white noise of naughty mahjong. But networked virtual mahjong was able to cut through the smut. "When I joined Sega, the company was best known for its *Virtua Fighter* fighting-game series," recalls *MJ* planner Katsuhiko Saito, "so *MJ* didn't exactly fit that kind of model. Since college, I've loved playing mahjong, and I see making mahjong games as my true calling."

Mahjong is not the only game of chance in Sega's amusement arsenal. In 2004, the company embarked on a collaboration with pachinko and pachi-slot maker Sammy to form Sega Sammy. Pachinko, a pinball-like game, can be found in the pachinko parlors that exist on almost every shopping street in Japan, but it is also a game center staple. Pachi-slot machines, also found in both

PACHINKO: A PINBALL-LIKE GAME

pachinko parlors and game centers, are similar to slot machines, but have a "skill-stop" button that allows the player to decide when to stop the spinning wheels. The Sega Sammy collaboration meant that *Virtua Fighter* got its own pachi-slot machine.

Like mahjong, pachinko's origins are foggy. The word "pachinko" has existed since the Meiji Era (1868–1912) and refers to something shot out of a catapult. "Pachinko" is the onomatopoeia for "slap" or "click," and *ko* means "ball." The game is believed to be derived from an American contraption called the Corinth Game, an upright version of pinball minus the flippers, which had players shoot metal balls in slots. Another theory attributes the game's origins to a surplus of metal ball bearings in Japan after World War I. Whatever the game's origins, the first pachinko parlor, >>>>>>>>

complete with wooden pachinko machines, opened in Nagoya in 1930. After the Second World War, the game's popularity boomed. In the immediate postwar years there was a cigarette shortage, and each adult was allotted only a handful. But with pachinko, it was possible to win tobacco, forever linking pachinko, cigarettes, and gambling. These days, machines in pachinko parlors pay

©GAINAX·カラー/Project Eva.

© GAINAX·カラー/Project Eva. © Bisty

NEON GENESIS EVANGELION PACHINKO AND PACHI-SLOT MACHINES

---

out metal balls, which can be exchanged for prizes, while game center machines pay out arcade coins or "medals," as they're called. These medals cannot be exchanged, but they can be used in medal-game machines.

Gone too are the days of simply watching spinning metal balls. Pachinko machines feature LCD displays in the middle of the pachinko machine that show anime or video-game characters, providing nothing more than visual stimulation. With pachinko and pachi-slot machines using video-game–quality scenes for their fifteen-inch LCD displays, pachinko companies aligning themselves with arcade-game makers makes sense. Though the tie-ups aren't always rosy. In 2001, Pachinko monolith Aruze Corp. bought out a then-struggling SNK and plundered the company's characters for its pachinko machines while neglecting the game division. "The arcade industry wasn't doing so well then," says an SNK employee. "Pachi-slot parlors were picking up, and it was trendy for young Japanese." Conditions got so bad for the arcade division that SNK

VIRTUA FIGHTER PACHI-SLOT AND PACHINKO MACHINES

founder Eikichi Kawasaki left the company with fellow SNK employees and created another company, Playmore. After Aruze drove SNK into the ground, Playmore successfully reacquired the rights to its characters and then sued Aruze for continuing to use those characters in its pachi-slot machines and won. SNK was reborn as SNK Playmore and still makes pachi-slot machines that feature SNK characters.

To make room for the newest pachinko and pachi-slot machines, parlors have a revolving door of inventory. Older machines find a home in arcades and are modified to accept and pay out worthless arcade coins that can only be used in medal-game machines. As far >>>>>>>

MJ4 CABINETS

SHE HITS A LARGE RED BUTTON THAT READS AGARI, LITERALLY MEANING "WIN." SHE'S GOT MAHJONG, AND SHE WINS THE GAME.

>>>>>>>>>> as Japanese arcade games come, they don't get any simpler than medal games. Players put medals in the large cabinets, in hopes of knocking down stacks of other medals in the machine. So easy that even children can play! And do. Game centers like Namco's Namco Land feature child-sized medal game cabinets targeted at grade schoolers. When housewife Emi Nishihana goes to the shopping mall with her family, her husband and two children make a beeline for Namco Land's medal-game section. Why do kids like medal games? Six-year-old Ku Nishihana replies, "Because you can win medals." Touché. That doesn't mean that hardened game center vets steer clear of medal machines. "I often play medal games," says *Virtua Fighter 5* director Daichi Katagiri. "I really dig them." The medal games that first appeared in Japanese arcades in the 1970s were usually imported Las Vegas casino games that had been altered to pay out medals instead of cash. The fact they dispensed medals put them in a gray area legally. Gambling is illegal in Japan, but medal games aren't technically gambling as players aren't winning money but worthless coins. Under Japanese law, players are not allowed to take the coins out of the arcades as they are actually the property of the game centers. Players must deposit their valueless arcade coins at the game center in special ATMs called

"medal banks," which even have biometric readers and require pin numbers! Even if medal games give players the winning sensation of gambling, medal games are simply "amusement machines" and not considered gambling.

Back in Kyoto, Haruka sits in front of *Sega Network Taisen Mahjong MJ4*, her fingers tapping the touchscreen, causing the virtual in-game hands to slap tiles on the green table. "Oh wow, this is really close," she says as the in-game announcers chirp, "Can the player pull it off?" A nearby flat-screen TV replays the game in real time. The screen in front of Haruka goes black, and she hits a large red button that reads *agari*, literally meaning "win." She's got mahjong, and she wins the game. "It's not the same feeling as winning in real mahjong, and beating the players sitting across from you," she says. Perhaps, though, this is one of the reasons why virtual mahjong is becoming more popular than actual mahjong. "Once you start losing in real mahjong, you're stuck sitting at that table with those three other players no matter how uncomfortable or disappointed you feel," says Haruka. "But in arcade mahjong, you don't have to sit it out with real people and you can just quit the game and leave the arcade. You're only out a few hundred yen, so no biggie." It's not real gambling after all. ✿

SEGA NETWORK TAISEN MAHJONG MJ4

THE WEIGHT OF *A GUN* IN YOUR HAND.

The thrill of sitting behind a wheel. The feeling of flying. If there's one thing that has continually worked in the favor of game centers in their fight to pry players away from home consoles, it's that often, arcades are able to offer an experience that simply couldn't be replicated with just a video screen, a joystick, and some buttons. Called "dedicated cabinets," these games are housed in specific casing and are built especially for a specific arcade experience. Driving games have steering wheels, flying games have flight sticks, and gun-shooting games have mock guns. "With arcade games, the cabinet is the most important thing. When you see a cabinet, that's

P1　P2

LIFE

THE HOUSE OF THE DEAD 4 SPECIAL

P1　P2

ヤバイ！つかまれる！

LIFE

usually when you decide whether you want to play a game or not," says Sega's arcade-game designer Yu Suzuki. "The form is the most important thing when you buy a car, right?" Right. Suzuki knows what he's talking about. He didn't invent the dedicated arcade cabinet, but he sure as hell perfected it. So feel free to judge these games by their covers.

"When I was very young, there weren't any video games," says the forty-nine-year-old Suzuki. Before the advent of video games, there

> **"THE CABINET IS THE MOST IMPORTANT THING. WHEN YOU SEE A CABINET, THAT'S USUALLY WHEN YOU DECIDE WHETHER YOU WANT TO PLAY A GAME OR NOT."**

YU SUZUKI

were mechanical games with cabinets designed for the particular game they housed and that game alone. Instead of running on a computer CPU, these mechanical games had motors, pulleys, levers, and blinking lights. Manufactured up until the end of the 1970s, the electronic circuitry of electromechanical games was primitive and simple. The machines were unreliable and broke down like crazy—either the mechanical parts or the electrical circuits or both. From "love testers" to animatronic fortune-tellers, these coin-operated games fill the evolutionary gap between old-fashioned carnival games like the ring toss, and modern video games. In Japan, the mechanical, pinball-like game pachinko has been popular since it first appeared as a fairground attraction in the 1920s. There was an explosion of pachinko parlors in the 1930s, but they were shuttered during World War II. The postwar era not only saw the reopening of the pachinko parlors, but also the laying of the foundations for modern Japanese game centers.

Jukeboxes, pinball, and GIs
with cash. American businessmen Martin Bromely, Irving
Bromberg, and James Humpert
had founded the company Standard Games in Hawaii in 1940
to provide entertainment for
military servicemen stationed
overseas, and they sensed an
opportunity in postwar Amer-
ican-occupied Japan. It was
in 1951 that the company
moved to Tokyo, complete with
name change. Standard Games
became the more descrip-
tive Service Games of Japan
(SErvice GAmes = Sega, ged-
dit?), and the following year
began importing pinball
machines into Japan. Later, in

SEGA'S FIRST BIG HIT, *PERISCOPE*

1965, the company would merge with Rosen Enterprises, another
Tokyo-based company, founded by American David Rosen, but one
that produced coin-operated photo booths, to become Sega Enterprises. The start-up continued importing pinball machines and made
some forays of its own into the mechanical games market with an
analog punching bag strength tester and a dome-covered analog
basketball game. In 1966, Sega exec Rosen designed the company's
first big hit, submarine simulator *Periscope*. The game had players
shoot cardboard ships with torpedoes made of light beams. State of
the art for the mid-1960s, *Periscope* featured realistic sound effects
and a periscope that players looked into while playing, all wrapped
in a huge dedicated cabinet that dwarfed even pinball machines.
This was the closest a civilian could get to torpedoing military ships!
Popular in places like smoky Japanese bowling alleys, *Periscope* was
inevitably exported to the US, where the coin box was altered to
accept quarters, making it the first twenty-five-cent-powered arcade ⟫⟫⟫⟫⟫⟫

game and setting the American arcade pricing that would last until the mid-1980s when games started costing two quarters a play.

In the late sixties and early seventies, Sega cranked mechanical games out of its Tokyo HQ. There was *Missile* (1969), which let players fire—you guessed it—missiles at planes projected on a screen. *Stunt Car* (1970) was a curious steering-wheel racing game cross-pollinated with pinball, where the point was to hit plastic balls

off the car's front bumper into slots for points. *Gun Fight* (also 1970) was a cowboy shoot-out where two miniature cowboys in a Dodge City–type diorama tried to pop electronic bullets in each other while taking cover behind adobe walls. The game's controls were realistically painted pistol

WHEN SHOT, THE PLASTIC COWBOYS WOULD FALL OVER, BUT THEN AUTOMATICALLY RISE UP WITHIN SECONDS FOR MORE COWBOY SHOOTIN'

SEGA'S *GUN FIGHT*

butts with working triggers. When shot, the plastic cowboys would fall over, but then automatically rise up within seconds for more cowboy shootin'. It was even possible to shoot off the tops of cacti. Extra lives and destructible environments!

By the end of the decade, mechanical games were dead as disco. The fatal blows were dealt by the one, two, three punch of Atari's *Pong*, and Taito's *Gun Fight* and *Space Invaders*. When Atari introduced *Pong* in the US in 1972, a few cabinets made their way to Japan. Throughout the decade, video games began replacing mechanical games in arcades across the

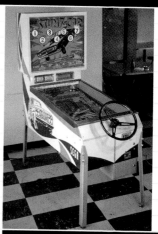

SEGA'S *STUNT CAR*

PLAYER 7

NAME: YU SUZUKI
SPECIALTY: DEDICATED CABINETS
**FAVORITE GAME: ANYTHING REALISTIC,
WITH A KNOCK-'EM-DEAD CABINET**

Famous as the brains behind legendary arcade games, *Space Harrier*, *Hang-On*, *Out Run*, and *Virtua Fighter*, gaming wasn't always a vocation for top game designer Yu Suzuki. Instead of spending his youth in bowling alleys playing mechanical games, he grew up building plastic models. Young Yu would buy cars and robots and then make totally new creations out of all the parts. He dreamt of becoming a dentist or a rock guitarist, and he still loves Van Halen. A Peavey Wolfgang guitar stands in the corner of his big, messy office with a desk covered in laptops and cables. But after seeing that his buddies were better rockers than he and failing the dental school examination, Suzuki asked around, trying to find a secure job. "People kept saying that the future was in computers. So in my third year at university, I started studies in programming," he says. "For me, programming was a bit like those plastic models—you could make anything." The fresh-faced college graduate started looking for computer programming work, applying to electronics companies. Gaming wasn't even a blip on his radar. "It had never been a particular ambition of mine to work for Sega, but during the interview, I started thinking that this company really looked interesting," he recalls. "That was when I decided to join." Beside arcade games, Suzuki created Sega console title *Shenmue*, which at seventy million dollars, is one of the biggest-budgeted video games ever.

OUT RUN, AN EARLY YU SUZUKI CREATION

country, culminating in the national hundred-yen-coin shortage induced by *Space Invaders*. Recalls Yu Suzuki, "Like the first car, the first motorcycle, the first rocket, *Pong* was the first arcade video game, and so this has a lot of importance. When I first saw it, for me it was like something straight out of the world of science fiction. It felt very fresh. The monitor wasn't so great, there was motion blur, so it had its problems, but it was still very important." Compared to mechanical games with their levers, cranks, and pulleys, video games didn't seem futuristic, they *were* futuristic! Still, the waves Atari made with *Pong* in 1972 were ripples compared to the tsunami created by Taito's *Space Invaders*. Like Sega, Taito was founded by a foreigner, Michael Kogan, a Russian Jew who had escaped the 1917 revolution, and was educated at Tokyo's Waseda University. Kogan created the Taito Trading Company, which started off much like Sega, importing and distributing jukeboxes and making mechanical games like strength

PLAYERS SAT IN A DEDICATED CABINET AND STEERED THEIR FORMULA ONE CAR THROUGH FUJI SPEEDWAY

testers or analog sports titles like *Basketball* (late 1960s), where the goal was to get a plastic ball into a hoop. By 1975, Taito had begun making arcade video games, such as its own cowboy shooting-game, also called *Gun Fight*, which featured two virtual quick-draw cowboys. The dual-joystick game was the first video game to use a microprocessor and the first Japanese video game that was exported to America. Taito was on a roll, and when it released *Space Invaders*, the entire country was hypnotized. *Space Invaders*, though, wasn't completely new. It was based on a 1972 Taito mechanical game, *Space Monsters*.

By the early 1980s, the video-game industry was exploding. In 1982, Suzuki entered Sega's R&D division as a programmer. The following year, he released his first game, a completely forgettable home console title called *Champion Boxing*. It was a trial run for his next title and first arcade game, *Hang-On*. Japanese game centers would never be the same.

In 1985, Sega didn't have a moneymaking arcade racing game. Competitor Namco (now known as NBGI) did. The game was Formula One–themed *Pole Position*. Players sat in a dedicated cabinet and steered their Formula One car through Fuji Speedway. It wasn't the first arcade racer: there'd been wheel-controlled mechanical racers since the 1960s and Atari introduced a black-and-white arcade video game called *Night Driver* in 1976. But the combination of the deluxe *Pole Position* cabinet and color graphics was

POLE POSITION

©NBGI

pretty dazzling for its day.

Pole Position's Formula One cars exploding into a fireball on impact was pretty neat, too. Around since the mid-fifties, Namco wasn't new to arcade gaming. The company got its start creating mechanical amusement rides found in small amusement areas on the rooftops of Japanese department stores, which were (and still are) places where parents could take bored kids for breaks while shopping. After acquiring the Japanese Atari branch in 1974, Namco focused more and more on those coin-eating arcade games, busting open the floodgates with its own invention *Pac-Man* in 1980.

"Sega's president kept asking why we didn't have a good driving game, so I decided to challenge myself by trying to make one," recalls Suzuki. "Since Namco's driving game was based on Formula One, I thought it would be childish for us to try and make another Formula One game." Race cars were out, and Suzuki came up something better: motorbikes. A longtime fan of motorcycles and Grand ⟫⟫⟫⟫⟫⟫

Prix racers like prodigy "Fast Freddie" Spencer, he explains: "I loved the GP 500 Spencer racer, so that's what I decided to recreate." The result was more than the Sega president could have ever expected. Suzuki created a deluxe dedicated cabinet with a slightly smaller-than-life-size motorcycle for players to sit on. It weighed over five hundred pounds! The game's monitor was embedded in the faux-bike cabinet, and instead of the been-there-done-that of simply turning the handlebar, *Hang-On* had motion controls. Want to go right? Lean right. Want to go left? Lean left. Sure, *Hang-On* used the same behind-the-vehicle perspective as *Pole Position*, with prettier graphics. But unlike the stationary *Pole Position*, Suzuki's *Hang-On* was actually moving!

In 1985, the same year *Hang-On* burned virtual rubber through Japanese arcades, a group of game execs got together for a pow-wow. The industry needed a standard arcade platform. Until then, each company had their own idea how the game should be wired to the cabinets, causing arcade gaming to move in a gazillion different directions. *Donkey Kong* and *Pac-Man*, for example, weren't wired in the same way, making it impossible for arcade owners to switch-swap games. They had to change cabinets.

That's where JAMMA comes in. The Japan Amusement Machinery Manufacturers' Association, to give the organization its full title, is a trade association that provides support and guidance to the industry through activities such as research on the standardization of technologies, and an annual game convention, the Amusement Machine Show, which acts a popular showcase for upcoming games from participating manufacturers. In 1985, the JAMMA standard was created. Before this, the game and the system board found inside the gaming cabinet were one and the same, with the game's circuits integrated within the board. Every cabinet was a dedicated cabinet! This meant

SUZUKI CREATED A DELUXE DEDICATED CABINET WITH A SLIGHTLY SMALLER-THAN-LIFE-SIZE MOTORCYCLE FOR PLAYERS TO SIT ON. IT WEIGHED OVER 500 POUNDS!

that when a game-center owner wanted to change games, he had to replace the whole damn thing, kit and caboodle. With the JAMMA standard, which took the form of a fifty-six-pin connector, the game's printed circuit board, or PCB, would be separate, and could be attached to any cabinet that was fitted with the JAMMA system board, similar to the way a player inserts a cartridge or disc at home on his console. All arcades needed was a cabinet casing, and the games could be changed out. Arcade gaming became much easier, cheaper, and ultimately more profitable for owners. >>>>>>>>

The JAMMA PCB's fifty-six pins controlled every aspect of the game, from power and video connections to all the controls and buttons, and even the coin mechanism. In the mid-eighties, games were still limited: one four-directional joystick and three play buttons per player, and only one speaker. Modifications were made to the boards by certain makers, usually to add a few more controls or so that a game could support stereo sounds. These PCBs, known as JAMMA+ or "pinout" (because they added more pins), would be made up of an original JAMMA board to which more connectors were added. Capcom's *Street Fighter II* used a JAMMA+ board, adding two extra nine-pin connectors for the three additional kick buttons used in the game. The game would still play if placed in a

REALER THAN REAL

Virtual reality! Japanese arcades were not immune to the 1990s buzzwords. In 1998, Atlus' *Amuse Vision Ride* provided a fully realized virtual experience, with images based on real-world photography instead of just graphics. Strapped into their seats, players donned a headset that provided a 3-D visual experience, with added sensations provided by the headset's stereo speakers and the cabinet itself, which would move along with the ride. Several scenarios were available, from roller coaster rides to descents of grand rapids, which could be enhanced with a few add-ons, such as a fan that blew wind on the body, or vibrations that made the seats shake. At the 2008 All Nippon Amusement Machine Operators' Union game show, two-hour lines showed the popularity of

Sega's *Mini Rider 2*. Billed as a "VR simulator," two people can sit inside the suspended podlike cockpit, with an inverted motion system providing an unprecedented and "moving" experience. The virtual rides offered

MINI RIDER 2: RE-CREATING REALITY

regular JAMMA cabinet without using the extra connectors, but players would have to deal with gimped versions of Ryu or Ken, since they wouldn't be able to do things like jab or roundhouse! It was also possible to get most non-JAMMA PCBs to work inside a JAMMA cabinet by using a specific adapter that could be either bought or, for the more enterprising owner, built.

But JAMMA wasn't the only system board. Although many companies continued to use the JAMMA standard, a few later developed their own boards: Capcom came up with the CPS-2 and Sega developed the NAOMI. While JAMMA's system helped create an organized, unified gaming platform (something console gaming doesn't have), it didn't work with dedicated cabinets that were designed for one >>>>>>>>

by the system include four scenarios, from glacier runs to cosmic journeys, which are enhanced by a giant forty-inch monitor.

Upping the bar is *Kido Senshi Gundam: Senjo no Kizuna*, or *Mobile Suit Gundam: Bonds of the Battlefield*, released by Namco Bandai Games Inc. (NBGI) in 2006, where you do more than just control fighting robots on-screen: you actually step into the cockpit to be fully immersed in your role as pilot. The game is of course based on popular animated series and Japanese institution *Gundam*. "Work on the game began in about 2002," recalls NBGI's Junichiro Koyama, "but the game's development has been in my mind since I was a boy." Inside the pod, players are confronted with a floor-to-ceiling cockpit view, and

there are surround-sound speakers to keep them in the moment as they grab the controls and battle with players in nearby pods, or anywhere in the country, thanks to the game's network play. The shape of the patented dome screen is elliptical, rather than round (which would make it difficult for players to see the bottom of the screen). The game has been so popular that NBGI has even incorporated a reservation system, the first arcade game to do so, so that folks can arrange times that they'd like to play in advance. "The cabinet, the game's development—everything was expensive," Koyama points out. "That's why it's expensive to play." The pilot card that you need to play the game costs three hundred yen; one round of *Senjo no Kizuna* is five hundred yen.

specific game. That's not to say companies like Sega, who specialized in dedicated cabinets, were against JAMMA. Heck, no! Sega execs sat (still do) on the JAMMA board of directors. Still, a line was drawn on the arcade linoleum floors, separating dedicated cabinet and non–dedicated cabinet games.

With Japan going gaga over Tom Cruise's *Top Gun*, Suzuki responded with F-14 Tomcat dog fighter *After Burner* (1987). While

SUZUKI WAS TAKING THE IDEA OF A CABINET AND RUNNING WITH IT, GIVING PLAYERS AN ARCADE EXPERIENCE

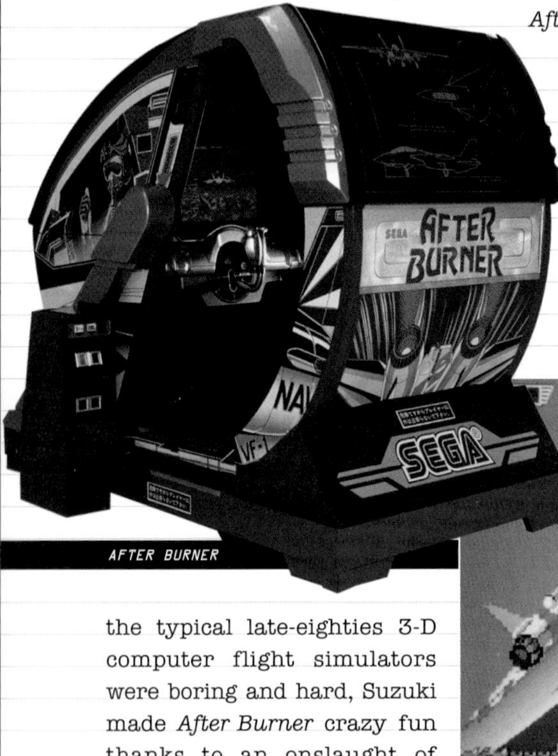

AFTER BURNER

AFTER BURNER

the typical late-eighties 3-D computer flight simulators were boring and hard, Suzuki made *After Burner* crazy fun thanks to an onslaught of missiles from enemy planes. Did it matter if gameplay was repetitive? Not at all, there were 'splosions! It was less a game, more a ride. Suzuki was taking the idea of a cabinet and running with it, giving players an arcade experience. Like most Sega cabinets of the decade, there were two versions: simple stand-up (SD) and sit-down deluxe (DX). The stand-up cabinet was reminiscent of earlier mechanical flying games like

Sega's *Jet Rocket* (1970), which had plane-style controls and a large one-minute clock that ticked off the sixty seconds of allotted gameplay. The sit-down *After Burner* was insane. The hydraulic cabinet moved up and down, while the seat was able to swing right and left, physically simulating flying a fighter plane. Inside, there was a flight seat, while

G-LOC

an in-game voice kept screaming "Fire! Fire!" Compared to other computer flight simulators, *After Burner* was hardly realistic and neither was Suzuki's air combat title *G-LOC* (1990), the spiritual successor to the *After Burner* series. A year later, Suzuki and his team released an *R-360 G-LOC* gyroscope-shaped dedicated cabinet that spun players all around and upside down. The game featured an "Experience Course" where folks would ride the cabinet without playing the game. The cabinet sported a roller coaster–style safety bar, had an emergency stop button should the *R-360* turn into a vomit comet, and even required a safety attendant. While the game wasn't very realistic, the nauseous feelings it induced were!

"'Real' is actually not the best word to use with games," Suzuki says. "You can't let 'real' get in the way of a good game." For Suzuki, "realistic" and "real" are very different. "If you play a five-minute action game, or you watch a two-hour movie, that's not reality. >>>>>>>>>

I don't need 'real,' but I very much need 'realistic.'" His first stab at arcade racing was *Out Run* (1986), which was actually more of a driving game than a racing game. Players cruised around in a Ferrari Testarossa convertible, a road car that reeked of yuppies, with a blonde chick in the passenger seat. The Testarossa didn't explode into a fireball like in *Pole Position*'s F1 crashes, but instead spun out and flipped over, throwing the driver and passenger out. The deluxe dedicated cabinet moved side to side (of course!), shook like hell during collisions,

"REAL" IS ACTUALLY NOT THE BEST WORD TO USE WITH GAMES. YOU CAN'T LET "REAL" GET IN THE WAY OF A GOOD GAME.

FERRARI F355 CHALLENGE

and the game featured this innovation: a radio that let players select from one of three soundtracks at the game's start. Few games summed up the decade better than *Out Run*. Ferrari-owner Suzuki later went on to create a race sim called *Ferrari F355 Challenge*, released in 1999. One version of the cabinet used three monitors, so that players could have a full panoramic view as they raced around the tracks. The cabinet featured three foot-pedals, and the game ran on four separate NAOMI boards. "It's more of a simulator and less of a game," says Suzuki. To make sure the game was real as possible, he used sensors to record car data, got input from Formula One, and even rented out the Fuji Speedway. The end result was so close to actual racing that the Ferrari Formula One team used the game for practice during the off-season. "The only difference between *Ferrari F355 Challenge* and *Out Run*," says Suzuki, "is the level of reality." In the late nineties, Sega rolled out actual life-size fiberglass car shells for selected Sega Joypolis arcades.

When *Hang-On* was a hit, Suzuki was surprised. When *Out Run* was a hit, Suzuki was surprised. When *After Burner* was a hit, blah, blah, blah. "*Virtua Cop* was the only game I was certain would be a big success," he says. The cabinet featured plastic pistols that players had to wield, tapping into a long-established staple: games with handheld guns. From cork-firing guns, BB guns, or actual gun guns, firearms in carnival-type bulls-eye games are nothing new.

VIRTUA COP

Mechanical penny arcade games with mounted pistols appeared as early as the 1920s in the United States. By the 1930s, American jukebox maker Seeburg created the first "light-gun" mechanical games. Seeburg's *Ray-O-Lite* rifle fired a beam of light at targets wired with sensors. Light-gun video games like *Virtua Cop* worked in reverse: the onscreen target emitted light, and pulling the light-gun's trigger allowed light to strike the photodetector in the gun's barrel. Mechanical light-gun game cabinets required a fifteen- to twenty-foot space between the target and the gun, while the video-game versions could be played up close—even with the light gun touching the cathode-ray screen.

The inspiration for *Virtua Cop* (1994), according to Suzuki, was the Clint Eastwood flick *Dirty Harry*, and a popular ad for canned coffee. *Dirty Harry*, fair enough, but a canned coffee ad? The TV spot showed a can of coffee growing bigger and bigger in a gun's sight. "When I saw that, I thought, yeah, you have to shoot the target before it gets to full size," he says. "So I wanted to use this ⟩⟩⟩⟩⟩⟩⟩⟩

HEAD TO HEAD

One thing all early eighties racing games like *Pole Position* and *Hang-On* had in common? They were single player. Either you could race against the computer or, well, that was pretty much it! While fighting games since 1984's *Karate Champ* let gamers go head-to-head, racing games didn't do that until Namco's *Final Lap* in 1987. The first arcade game to incorporate linked network play, *Final Lap* let up to eight drivers race F-1 cars simultaneously on Japan's Suzuka Circuit track. While not a direct sequel, the game is a follow-up to Namco's earlier *Pole Position*. "The genesis of *Final Lap* was wondering how it would be to play *Pole Position* against human opponents," says game designer Tatsuro Okamoto. "I thought the more cabinets we were able to link, the more exciting the race would be, but I finally estimated that eight cabinets were the maximum for the arcade environment." Close enough to smack talk!

© NBGA

FINAL LAP

kind of system, and I thought it would be popular." And Suzuki thinks the game's mass appeal also has parallels with virtual pet Tamagotchi. Tamagotchi? Bear in mind that *Virtua Cop* is part of a genre referred to as "rail shooters," since players have no control over where they go in the game, and simply shoot at whatever new obstacle is put in front of them. This, says Suzuki, is where Tamagotchi comes in. "With Tamagotchi, the player doesn't have any freedom. You have to listen to what it says, you have to clean up after it. Some people want to be able to make decisions, but others are very comfortable taking orders. My wife never asks me what I want to eat. She just says eat this, eat this, eat this . . . There hadn't really been any games where you didn't have to think. I believe that's why Tamagotchi became so popular. And I think that's one of the reasons for the success of *Virtua Cop*."

Virtua Cop's success led to an arcade gun-game renaissance, with Namco and Konami both churning out solid shooting games. The light gun for Namco's *Time Crisis* (1995) featured a realistic blowback recoil that snapped! The game also had a foot pedal, which when pressed would cause the on-screen character to take cover. Konami ditched the foot pedal and used motion sensors for *The Keisatsukan: Shinjuku Cop 24 Hours* (known as *Police 911* in America), released in 2001, forcing players to physically crouch and dodge virtual bullets. And it doesn't get more immersive than Sega's 2006 release *The House of the Dead 4 Special*, ▸▸▸▸▸▸▸▸

THE HOUSE OF THE DEAD 4 SPECIAL

a souped-up version of the horror zombie shooting game, in which players were fully immersed in an enclosed space, sitting down on force-feedback chairs with safety bars that could rotate to face one of two 100-inch monitors placed both in front and in back of players.

This isn't the playing pinnacle—we're just getting started, folks. Suzuki says arcade gaming can do more. Much, much more. "Cell phones are popular," he points out. "Maybe that could be a game controller." Of better yet, what about your arm? Yes, your arm. "It doesn't have to be a scary thing, but you could put a sensor here," Suzuki says, pointing to his arm. This isn't the future—some

CRAZY CABINETS

Hard to believe, but there's more to life than shooting guns, driving race cars, and flying jet planes! Want to skim the waves on a personal watercraft? Hop onto *Aqua Jet* (1996) from Namco (now known as NBGI) and take a ride on the jet-ski replica that formed most of the cabinet. Better yet, Sega's jet-ski simulator *Wave Runner* (also 1996) had the body of an actual Yamaha jet ski. Feeling like some white river rapids? With Namco's *Rapid River* (1997), you sat inside a partial raft, and maneuvered your boat with paddle-shaped controls in front of a fifty-inch screen. Think fishing is exciting? It's not! Still, Sega came out with hook-line-and-sinker *Get Bass* (1998), which had a vibrating fishing-reel controller. Namco's *Prop Cycle* (1996) was a prop-plane flying game powered by an actual exercise bike! If trains are your thing, then Taito's *Densha de Go!* (1996), and its many sequels, gave you the train throttle controls of city trains or trams from actual service routes in Japan. Sega's *18 Wheeler: American Pro Trucker* (2000) put you behind the wheel and in the guise of a CB-radio-chattin' trucker, racing cross-country with cargo in tow, and *Top Skater* (1997) featured a moveable skateboard that players moved right and left, while

JET SKIING IN A TOKYO GAME CENTER

people are already chipped for medical reasons, which isn't quite on the same level as arcade gaming. "If for some that would be a bit too scary, then you could also do something simpler, like using a wristband or a pendant," he says. Or what about life-size monitors with life-size in-game characters? Or hi-tech directional speakers so that one player can hear what's said, while the other player can't? Or arcade games that can be controlled by the mind? At forty-nine years old, Suzuki is still buzzing with new concepts. "Ideas come from everywhere, and I have lots of great ideas for cabinets, but I always have to deal with cost," he says. "If money wasn't an issue, just think of the cabinets I could make!" ✪

holding onto safety bars for support. At the 2008 All Nippon Amusement Machine Operators' Union expo, Sega exhibited *Kingyo Sukui*, a re-creation of a popular festival game in which children try to catch goldfish with flimsy paper scoops. In the game, which looks like a garishly decorated festival stall, up to four players sit around a large video screen that faces up, representing the pool. Using a joystick, players move their virtual scoop around the screen, trying to catch fish.

Dedicated cabinets can bring new realism to all kinds of crazy. Like hitting people on the head and sticking your finger up people's bottoms. Case in point, Namco's *Nice Tsukkomi* (2002), in which the player makes up one half of a comedy duo performing a *manzai* routine—a popular form of stand-up comedy in Japan that involves two comedians. First, you choose a pairing with one of nine partners. Then, standing next to your dummy partner, you play the straight man (*tsukkomi*) to your partner's funny man (*boke*), dealing him blows and smacks. It's all about timing, as you would expect with comedy, with the proper hit to various body parts contributing to your score. But the most infamous arcade cabinet isn't Japanese. *Boong-ga Boong-ga*, ("Spank 'em") was a game released in 2000 by Korean company Taff System for the Korean and Japanese markets. The game features a controller in the shape of a probing finger, which you insert in the cabinet's built-in posterior. The *kancho*, a Japanese slang word for the act (literally meaning "enema"), is a popular prank among schoolchildren—the Japanese equivalent of the "wedgie."

THESE AREN'T JUST OLD ARCADE GAMES, BUT MEMORIES.

They're "retro." A loose way of referring to older, classic titles that span the late 1970s to the early 1990s. Whether it's two colorful *Bubble Bobble* dragons using bubbles to save their girlfriends or a shirtless mayor giving punks knuckle sandwiches in *Final Fight*, the pixelated graphics are lo-res compared to twenty-first-century home consoles. But even with retro titles popping up on everything from home consoles and PC emulators to portable consoles and cell phones, these vintage titles still draw players to retro game centers not only to play, but to pay to play. To sit down in front of musty, cigarette-burned arcade cabinets and shell out coins, not for a new experience, but to relive an old one.

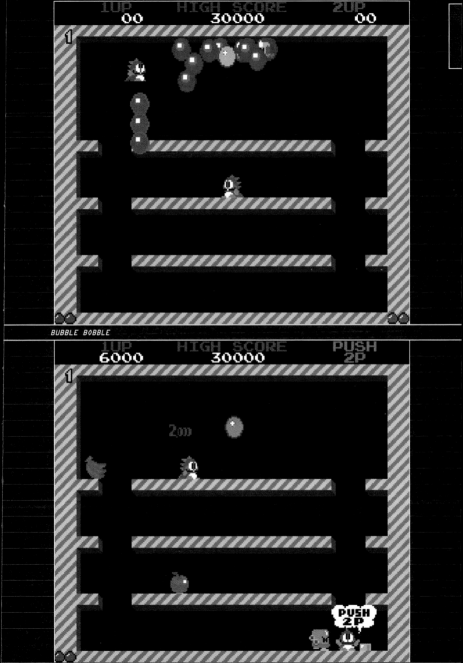

FINAL FIGHT, CAPCOM'S 1989 BEAT 'EM UP

>>>>>>>>>> "When I was young, I remember my local game center sold really good hot dogs and ice-cream," recalls Tokyo-based game designer Goichi Suda, the brains behind *killer7* (2005) for the Nintendo Game-Cube, and the delightfully lurid *No More Heroes* (2007) for the Wii, "and sometimes that comes back to me if I walk into a game center." It was the late 1970s, and Goichi Suda was in third grade. Taito's *Space Invaders* had just come out, causing the Japanese arcade scene—previously dominated by mechanical games like pinball and Atari *Pong* clones—to explode. After baseball practice, Suda would sneak off by himself to the bowling alley in his hometown of Nagano. The entrance of the bowling alley was packed with arcade games: postwar analog arcade games

"I WANT TO PUT THAT RETRO ATMOSPHERE INTO THE GAMES THAT I CREATE"

GOICHI SUDA

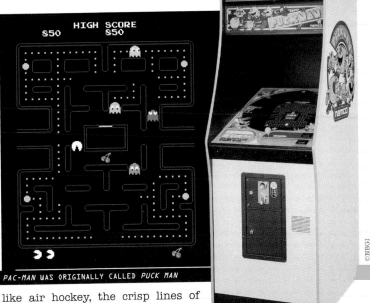

PAC-MAN WAS ORIGINALLY CALLED *PUCK MAN*

like air hockey, the crisp lines of Vectorbeam games, and of course *Space Invaders*. After *Space Invaders*, a rash of new video games appeared: Namco's shooter *Galaxian* in 1979, (the first true color arcade game), Namco's *Pac-Man* in 1980 (the first arcade-game character), and Nintendo's *Donkey Kong* in 1981 (the first arcade game with plot). Innovation after innovation followed and by 1982 the arcade revolution was in full swing. Players walked into their local game center and saw games the likes of which they'd never come across before. "I still have memories of when I first went to a game center, of how jaw dropping it was," recalls the forty-year-old Suda. "When I'd go to game centers, I'd get this feeling of discovering something entirely new. I try to bring this to my game design, to give players the same feeling that I had back then. I want to put that retro atmosphere into the games that I create."

Before the 1980s, Japan's game centers were dark places with glowing screens that burned bright with shooters and racing games. That is, until the one-two punch of *Pac-Man* and *Donkey Kong*. *Pac-Man* fever hadn't hit yet, and with game centers still called "invader houses," *Pac-Man* didn't quite fit the bill. No surprises that initially the yellow pellet-muncher got only a lukewarm response. Designed by Toru Iwatani of Namco (now NBGI), word has it the shape of the ⟩⟩⟩⟩⟩⟩⟩

iconic character was inspired by a pizza missing a slice. (Though Iwatani admitted in the 1980s that the character was also based on a rounded-out version of the Japanese character for "mouth"). Gameplay was straightforward and simple: players maneuvered pellet-munching Pac-Man through the maze, avoiding ghosts. By the mid-1980s, Pac-mania was gobbling up coins from Sapporo to Okinawa. A year later, along came *Donkey Kong*, from playing-card manufacturer Nintendo. Starring a mustached carpenter in red overalls named Jumpman, the game was the first arcade title to have, well, a jump button, as well as being the first platformer. Jumpman hopped over barrels, climbed ladders, and jumped from suspended platform to suspended platform as he tried to rescue a damsel from his pissed-off pet gorilla. The game was a smash, and sixty-five thousand cabinets were sold in Japan, propping up the then-struggling Nintendo and laying the groundwork for Nintendo and *Donkey Kong* creator Shigeru Miyamoto to dominate gaming throughout the 1980s

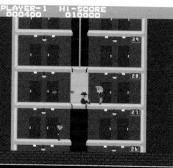

and beyond. For the *Donkey Kong* sequel, Jumpman would be renamed Mario, change his profession from carpenter to plumber, and eventually become gaming's own Mickey Mouse.

"I LOVE ELEVATOR ACTION," SAYS GOICHI SUDA. "I LOVE GAMES WITH STORIES."

ELEVATOR ACTION

The early eighties in Japan was the golden age of arcade gaming, but at the time parents and teachers couldn't have cared less. "Game centers had a bit of a bad image, a bad reputation—bad kids would often go there and hang out," says Suda. "My friends didn't want to go to those places, my parents didn't want me to go there, and even at school they told us not to go to game centers. But I wanted to be there." Like a moth drawn to a flame, young Suda kept his secret hidden and snuck to that smoky Nagano bowling alley arcade, populated with young hoods and ruffians. "I was careful not to bring too much money with me, in case they'd try to steal it," says Suda.

NAME: GOICHI SUDA
SPECIALTY: RETRO GAMES
FAVORITE GAME: ELEVATOR ACTION

Goichi Suda (aka Suda 51) first got his gaming chops writing wrestling games for Nintendo's Super Famicom home console. In his *Super Fire Pro Wrestling Special* (1994), the ending has the main character commit suicide offscreen by shooting himself, in a pop-culture reference to Kurt Cobain. Macabre and pulpy, sure, but nothing out of character for Suda, who before getting into game design was an undertaker. Even after he moved on from making straight-up wrestling titles to his killer-with-multiple-personalities game *killer7*, Suda would appear in publicity pics wearing a lucha libre mask. The CEO of his own independent studio Grasshopper Manufacture,

Suda focuses on home console games. His diverse influences—from Kafka, to *Jackass*, to Scorsese, to wrestling arcade title *WWF Superstars*—have made for wildly entertaining, critically acclaimed games like lightsaber hitman title *No More Heroes* for the Wii.

"I believe that games, as a medium, are works of art," Suda says. His games certainly go to prove it.

でもいいね…
バカでダメな男に弱いの

NO MORE HEROES

"But then again, I was just a kid, so I didn't really have much money anyway." And when he did have money, he was shoving coins in games like Taito's platformer *Elevator Action* (1983), which put players in the role of a spy that hops on elevators to move between floors, dodging baddies and bullets, to collect secret documents. "I love *Elevator Action*," he says. "I love games with stories."

Games were a hundred yen for one play. Older games were playable for the bargain-basement price of fifty yen. Still pricey if you were just a kid! While Atari ruled American arcades and home consoles during the late seventies and early eighties, Suda points out that not many Atari home machines were imported to Japan. Japanese kids had no choice really but to bring their stacks of coins to the local arcade. And when Suda didn't have enough money for games, he would swipe pocket change from his parents. But after befriending

RETRO SHOPPING

Tokyo's Akihabara district, also known as Electric Town for its concentration of stores selling electronic and computer goods, has in recent years been turning into a showcase for all things otaku—from anime to manga and everything in between—but it hasn't yet turned its back on its electronic origins, especially when it comes to gaming. In an inconspicuous corner building a few blocks from the station, you'll notice the green and yellow signs of G-Front, a shop that specializes in printed circuit boards (PCBs) for a variety of vintage, classic, and hard-to-get-hold-of games. Walk up to the second floor store, grab the price list at the door, and then take in the scene: rows and rows of

PCBs, most of them packaged in blue bubble wrap, filling up every inch of shelf and floor space, a treasure trove of retro arcade gaming. As

the tough arcade kids, the future video-game designer picked up game-center cheats like hot-wiring cabinets with cigarette lighters so that they would dish out free games. "You could also take a five-yen coin," says Suda, "and with cellophane tape try to make it feel ridged like a fifty-yen coin, and then use that." All of this right under the noses of arcade clerks! When you're ten years old, and you've already spent all your lunch money blowing through round after round of *Space Invaders*, ya gotta do what ya gotta do. Tough kids skipping school and sneaking cigs was arcade culture—there were none of the sanitized family fun centers prevalent today, with nothing but kiddy card games and crane-game machines. "I'm not really satisfied with arcade culture these days," says Suda. "Before, it was more underground, quite different from what you have now." That's exactly where Shibuya Kaikan Monaco comes in. >>>>>>>>>>

well as the boards to go inside the arcade cabinet, you can buy display signs to put on top of the cabinet, instructions for the game, spare wires, buttons, and joysticks (you'll even spot a few cabinets too). Prices vary greatly, from just a few thousand yen to quite a bit more. There's hard-to-find titles like Namco's last

8-bit title *Wonder Momo* (1987), a beat 'em-up starring panty-flashing super heroine Momo, for 71,400 yen or Sega's super-rare, super-expensive maze shooter *Tranquilizer Gun* (1980), which had little green hunters shoot tranquilizers into wild animals like gorillas, elephants, and lions. While *Tranquilizer Gun* will set you back 207,900 yen, there are deals to be had, like developer Dimps' brilliant 2-D fighting game *The Rumble Fish* (2004) for a mere 5,000 yen. The clientele is a mix of game-center operators and gaming enthusiasts, who either come to buy boards, or to trade in their old ones. So if you're thinking of starting your own personal retro arcade, G-Front is the place to go.

SHIBUYA KAIKAN MONACO

Take the Hachiko exit at Shibuya station, fight your way over the city's most congested pedestrian scramble crossing, then down Center-gai, the narrow shopping street to the left of the towering Q-Front building (home to one of the world's busiest Starbucks). You'll soon find yourself standing in front of what could be described as a retro gaming shrine, or a museum, even. To the right of the entrance, on the black cement exterior, there's white graffiti-like lettering proudly proclaiming: "1 PLAY ¥50." Just on top of that, in Japanese: "Video Games, 230 Machines." This is it, here we go, Shibuya Kaikan Monaco.

Sickly green walls and ruby red mats lead the way up four floors of retro-gaming goodness. Players plop down on black-cloth-covered stools and shove coin after coin into off-white Capcom- and Sega-branded cabinets. Black electrical tape holds together the edge of one

YOU NAME IT, MONACO HAS IT: FIGHTING GAMES, SHOOTERS, RHYTHM GAMES, AND A COUPLE OF SIDE-SCROLLER BEAT 'EM UPS

INSIDE SHIBUYA KAIKAN MONACO

cabinet, while players tap red buttons like they're typing. You name it, Monaco has it: fighting games, shooters, rhythm games, and a couple of side-scroller beat 'em ups such as *Final Fight*, where the object is to win points by beating the tar out of hordes of random bad dudes with either fists or swords—elements of which Suda added to his Nintendo Wii console game *No More Heroes*. There's Capcom's 1991 medieval fantasy title *The King of Dragons*, where players can beat up dwarves and elves, or Capcom's 1993 comic-book-inspired beat 'em up *Cadillacs and Dinosaurs*, where players can beat up gun-toting bad guys and dinosaurs. There's Chinese-myth-inspired hack 'n' slash, meat-bun-eatin' *Tenchi wo Kurau II* (1992), known as *Warriors of Fate* in English, also from Capcom, who went beat 'em up bonkers and slashing silly in the early 1990s. While it can ▶▶▶▶▶▶▶

take hours to clear though a modern home-console game, players at Monaco can blow through these older games in less than fifteen minutes. There's no way to pause or save these retro titles, so the quicker, the better. But with the vast majority of retro games available on home consoles, why do players keep coming? "I see it sort of like the equivalent of movies, and the advent of videos and DVDs," says Suda. "Going to the movie theater is a different and more traditional experience than watching DVDs at home." There's no arguing that playing SNK's 1996 run-and-gun title *Metal Slug* in the comfort of one's home is far different from playing at a cabinet with a joystick and buttons, next to sweaty Monaco dudes with cigarettes dangling out of their mouths.

THE RISE OF THE HOME CONSOLE

Dead of summer 1983, the Famicom home console goes on sale in Japan. Better known as the Nintendo Entertainment System in the West, the 8-bit Famicom—short for "Family Computer"—was cartridge-based and was launched with home versions of Nintendo's coin-op games *Donkey Kong, Donkey Kong Jr.,* and *Popeye.* Since the American home consoles, like the Atari 2600 and the Magnavox Odyssey, never hit the Land of the Rising Sun in widespread numbers, the Famicom was very much a marvel in 1983. "I was just so amazed that you could play games and not have to pay for every play," recalls Goichi Suda. "It was a shock to be able to play for free at home!" He was probably relieved he didn't have to swipe coins from his parents or

hot-wire arcade machines anymore. The Famicom's popularity grew throughout the eighties, and in 1990 the upgraded Super Famicom was released. It wasn't until 2003 that Nintendo actually stopped manufacturing the machine! (And only stopped doing so because obtaining parts for its electric innards proved difficult.) Is Famicom

DONKEY KONG FOR THE FAMILY COMPUTER

Toshiyuki Kanbayashi knows Shibuya Kaikan Monaco. The forty-year-old manager has worked there for twenty years—"only a short time," answers Kanbayashi when posed the question. It all happened by accident. Kanbayashi was working as a regular salaryman, but didn't like his boss much and so decided to bail. While strolling around Tokyo one day, he noticed an ad for part-time work at a game center. "Since I really like games, I decided to go in for an interview, and that's when they suggested that I come work at Shibuya Kaikan Monaco." The rest, as they say, is arcade history. Kanbayashi loves games, and whether it's Namco's insanely hard maze-filled *The Tower of Druaga* (1984) or the latest Konami rhythm game, he's tuned in. You'd think managing a game center >>>>>>>>

retro? No, says Suda. "Retro is about the games that you could play at game centers, the games that I played when I was a kid. For me it really refers to the games that came out before the Famicom." The Famicom has more in common with modern game consoles than arcade machines. For instance, the Famicom could connect to the Internet via a huge add-on dial-up modem, making it the first connected home console. Unlike today's consoles, it didn't have online gaming, but could be used for online banking and stock trading! The Famicom controller also utilized a small microphone and introduced a directional pad and button layout that continues to influence modern home console controllers. Suda adds: "For people of my age, who grew up on arcade games, when Famicom first came out, it seemed to be mainly supported by a new, younger generation of gamers. I was already in high school." And into girls and stuff.

THE NINTENDO FAMILY COMPUTER

would be the ultimate dream job. Nope! "I don't play games here, and the same goes for the rest of the staff. We had some problems a while back with some employees playing while on duty," he explains. "That's why I go play games elsewhere." Monaco's staff don't really represent the "maniac" (a term Kanbayashi likes to use) gamer. "Of course, I don't think there's anyone who works here who hates playing games, but they don't tend to be huge gamers either. It's not the hard-core gamers who come looking for a job here." Problem solved.

The entire staff that keeps Monaco up and running, including Kanbayashi, numbers eight, with three on duty at any one time. "Since we need to cover all four floors, we're constantly moving around the center throughout the day." Not only does his day-to-day routine require him to cover all of the regular roles expected of a game center manager (opening and closing shop, welcoming customers, cleaning up, taking care of problems that may occur with customers, hiring new staff), it also includes one that is rather specific to Monaco and other retro arcades, and without a doubt one of the most important: machine specialist. As is to be expected when most of the games that fill up your center are quite old, maintenance is a key concern. A wipe down with a warm towel and disinfectant covers cabinet care. Gum tape is a last resort! "If it's a hardware problem, for example if a wire is broken or something like that, then I can often fix it myself," says Kanbayashi as he crouches in front of a cabinet, with the bottom panel door open, revealing the >>>>>

"IF A WIRE IS BROKEN OR SOMETHING LIKE THAT, THEN I CAN OFTEN FIX IT MYSELF"

TOSHIYUKI KANBAYASHI

KILL SCREENS

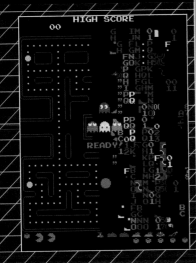

Early arcade games would continue to cycle through previous levels, based on the assumption that players wouldn't be good enough to, say, play *Pac-Man* for almost five hours straight and clear the 255th board. Ha, little did they know! Since there wasn't enough memory on the arcade circuit board, hitting the 256th *Pac-Man* board would cause the game to crash and the right half of the screen turn to a garbled mess of code. Put in the four hours plus of play to hit the 256th board on *Dig Dug* and watch as character Dig Dug dies over and over again. Likewise, Jumpman in *Donkey Kong* keels over and croaks when players reach the 22nd board.

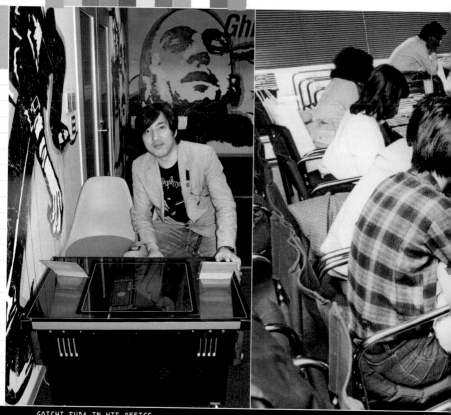

GOICHI SUDA IN HIS OFFICE

>>>>>>> machine's innards. There are limitations though. "If it's a software problem, then there's nothing much I can do."

Kanbayashi laughs at the notion of places like Monaco being compared to a museum. "A museum? Definitely not, there's no comparison. Although the building is pretty old!" He doesn't particularly see the need to give special status to these old game centers nor does he feel any urgency to preserve these games. "I don't think that what we have here is particularly rare or even that valuable. I think that a lot of the people that play these games just never stopped. They played them when they were young, and they carry on playing now because we are still offering them." According to Kanbayashi, it's not that Shibuya Kaikan Monaco decided to cater to the retro crowd, but that this aging arcade simply kept going.

EARLY "INVADER HOUSE"

Goichi Suda takes a more nostalgic view. "There aren't many places left where you can still play the old games," he says, wistfully. He's sitting in the lobby of his office, playing through *Street Fighter II*. The walls are covered with pop art, and the lobby has two tabletop cabinets. These are the same type of glass-topped cabinets that were found in every Invader House. Players would sit down, plunk a coin in, and set their glass of sugary milk-tea on the cabinet. "Retro arcade boards tend to be cheap, so we bought some for Grasshopper," Suda says. "I'd actually like to open a retro game center." He gets up from the tabletop cabinet and goes over towards the window. "I could even do it right over there," he says pointing to an empty lot. And you can bet there'd be soft serve ice-cream and delicious hot dogs.

CHAPTER 9
CARD-BASED GAMES

ゲー！

ゲームマン

カ500

TWO PASTIMES, CLEVERLY COMBINED.

Card-based arcade games, a mash-up of playing arcade games and collecting cards, are bringing a new generation of gamers into Japan's arcades. To play these games you need cards: cards printed with old-school bar codes, or cards embedded with smart chips. The cards contain data, which is scanned or swiped into the game. Either the cards load data into the game or the cards themselves act as game pieces that are moved on a flat smart-card reader causing the in-game counterparts to move in real time—card-pushing gameplay that looks more like analog tabletop gameplay. For a younger generation of players, this is what arcade gaming is all about. Put in money, collect a card (or cards), and play the game. Even if players lose, they still get more than a simple hi-score and the swagger of pride. They get cards. Lots of cards.

1P

ウルトラマン登場!!
<ruby>登場<rt>とうじょう</rt></ruby>

DAIKAIJYU BATTLE ULTRA MONSTERS EX

2644　　　　1970

アタック 1100　　　　アタック 1100

2　3　4　5

ディフェンス 700　◆◆◆ ボタンをおしまくれ！　ディフェンス 800

ARCADE GAMES FOR MINIATURE PLAYERS

>>>>>>>>>   Standing in line, five-year-old Ren opens his album filled with *Daikaijyu Battle Ultra Monsters EX* cards from Data Carddass, and carefully looks at each one. He's waiting to play the game of the same name. The cards feature monsters from the *tokusatsu* ("special effects") superhero TV show *Ultraman*. While the show focuses on the exploits of Ultraman as he pounds monsters destroying miniature Tokyo, this game has monsters beat the tar out of each other. Kids put in a hundred-yen coin, and the cabinet spits out a bar-coded card that the kids swipe in a card reader. Whatever appears on the card then appears in-game. The cabinets have two sets of three buttons for one- and two-player games, and kids pound away at them. The faster the button-mashing, the stronger the monster attack! "That always makes my hands hurt," says Ren. "A lot." Other arcade games for miniature players don't take such a beating, but are based on either timing, selecting powerful characters, or rock-paper-scissors.

    Blame the bugs. In arcades, the kiddy card-game craze started back in 2003 when Sega released *Mushiking: The King of Beetles*, which had this thrilling plot: a fairy in green duds and the King of Beetles try to protect the good bugs from the evil foreign bugs. The pint-size game cabinets dispensed cards that were swiped through

KIDS PUT IN A HUNDRED-YEN COIN, AND THE CABINET SPITS OUT A BAR-CODED CARD

a bar-code reader. In-game, the card's bug appeared on screen and kids could have virtual bugs fight via the game's rock-paper-scissors gameplay. Bug collecting has always been popular in Japan, with families spending weekends tromping through the woods hoping to find rare stag beetles that fetch insane prices at pet stores. Not everyone can go bug hunting. But everyone can play *Mushiking*. The game was a smash, inspiring an anime and a manga. By 2005, 160 million cards had been shipped, and between 2003 and 2007 over 100 thousand official Sega-held tournaments had taken place, earning the game a place in *The Guinness Book of World Records*. >>>>>>>>

DAIKAIJYU BATTLE CARDS AND CABINET

Since *Mushiking* was for boys (boys like bugs, apparently), Sega wised up and released a girly counterpart called *Love and Berry*. The game was based on choosing outfits for in-game characters and was so popular that a line of *Love and Berry* clothes was launched, letting girls choose real outfits. How's that for cross promotion!

But before *Mushiking*, there was another kiddy card-game craze. In 1995, Nintendo released a card game called *Pocket Monsters* that was later rebranded *Pokémon* abroad to avoid confusion with an American toy line called *Monster in My Pocket*. Players bought packs of cards with cute *Pokémon* characters and had them battle each other in a *War*-type non-arcade tabletop card game. Nintendo was no stranger to card games. In the late nineteenth century, the company, then known as Nintendo Playing Card Co., started making hand-painted flower-motif playing cards called *Hanafuda* and continues to do so. *Pokémon*'s creator Satoshi Tajiri based the game on his childhood memories of bug collecting. *Pokémon* did monster business worldwide, spawning an anime TV series, movies, and video games. But by the mid-1990s, Nintendo had long moved on from the arcade scene and the *Pokémon*

PLAYER 9

NAME: REN
AGE: FIVE
SPECIALTY: CARD GAMES
FAVORITE GAME: DAIKAIJYU BATTLE

HIGHEST SCORE: He's not playing for points, but cards.
FAVORITE MOVE: Button-mashing
RAREST CARD: Alien Baltan
MOST DUPLICATED CARD: Red King
MOST SOUGHT AFTER CARD: Ultraman Nice from *Daikaijyu Battle*
FAVORITE CARD: Zetton. He's really strong.

NUMBER OF CARDS COLLECTED:
Two hundred plus
GAMING AMBITIONS: "Dad, can we sell our home consoles so we can go to the arcade more?"

ZETTON: HE'S REALLY STRONG

video game was only released for consoles. In 2007, Nintendo licensed out *Pokémon* to Tomy and AQ Interactive, who came up with an arcade game that uses poker-like chips called pucks that are embedded with smart chips. "I never get any good pucks," says little Ren, whose collection is easily a hundred pucks plus. "Only ones I already have."

Card games aren't just for knee biters like Ren. In one corner of Ikebukuro's Sega Gigo game center, two players sit side by side at adjacent cabinets of *Sangokushi Taisen 3*, Sega's historical card game for adults. The player on the right reeks yakuza chic with his lightly shaded glasses and punch-perm hairstyle. His buddy's appearance is less blunt, but he still comes off as the type you'd normally see early morning waiting for a pachinko parlor to open. In the rain. With no umbrella. Nearby, two office ladies in their >>>>>>>

early twenties are sharing one seat in front of another cabinet, giggling their way through fierce battles with their armies. One of them gets up, goes to the nearby card vending machine, and drops a few coins to get a starter deck of cards for herself. Another player, in the ubiquitous, bland, navy blue suit of the Japanese salaryman, is busy expertly swiping cards across the play surface. He has a pile of cards to the side, which he browses through between matches, looking for a particular character, skill, or spell that will help him along the path to victory.

This mixed cross section of customers is typical of the card-based games section of the game center. Hit here on weekends, and there's long lines of players patiently lined up in cordoned areas, waiting for their chance to play. Unlike the kiddy barcode Data Carddass games, these large-cabinet card games use a flat-panel card reader that doubles as a play surface, over which cards for that particular game are placed, immediately recognized, and incorporated into the play session. In addition to the cards for a particular game, the player's data is stored on a smart

card inserted in a separate slot. Card-based games for adults first became popular in 2002 with the launch of Sega's *World Club Champion Football*, which remains one of the leading titles of the genre. Still in their infancy, card-based games represent the future of arcade games. "From now on, the number of card games will increase," says *Sangokushi Taisen* producer Yasuhiro Nishiyama. "We're entering a new era in arcade gaming."

Cards can be obtained by buying them, trading them, or winning them from the game machines. Each card has its own special powers and properties, and greatly affects the gameplay strategy. It's the ultimate case of customization in games, and the legion of nonelectronic collectible card games that have preceded these new arcade-based games have proven just how successful a formula it can be. Since cards are randomly given, it's sometimes difficult to get your hands on that one special card. Starter packs are sold via in-arcade vending machines. Another option is trading with friends

> **"FROM NOW ON, THE NUMBER OF CARD GAMES WILL INCREASE. WE'RE ENTERING A NEW ERA IN ARCADE GAMING."**

(or begging them for their doubles). For those without friends or without friends that game, some game centers even have notice boards for players to leave messages offering possible trades. And as with traditional collectible card games there also exists a very strong after-market for the cards. Step into any of Japan's hobby stores—selling all kinds of games from card and board games to pen-and-paper role-playing games and miniature tabletop war games—and next to the rows of glass showcases that sell cards for traditional, non-arcade games, you'll find a generous supply of cards for arcade-based games as well, ready to bleed you dry. There are also specialist card stores where you can trade in your old cards and buy other people's unwanted cards. >>>>>>>>>

Companies that make arcade card games won't comment on the secondary market that thrives in the world of collectible cards, but seeing as it's not something they actively try to stop, it seems that the value and attention it brings to the cards is certainly not lost on them.

The king of card games? Sega's massively popular *Sangokushi Taisen* series, released in 2005, and still putting asses in front of arcade cabinets. Set in the Three Kingdoms Era of Chinese history, the story—already featured in countless novels and manga and endless *Dynasty Warriors* home video games—covers a period of turmoil in the third century AD that saw the demise of the Han dynasty and the fight for power that

SANGOKUSHI TAISEN CARD

ensued. Thrilling! "Personally, I love the Three Kingdoms Era," says Nishiyama. "There are countless great characters and fascinating stories." Nishiyama isn't alone. The rich setting, with its expansive martial canvas of intrigue and standout personalities has attracted many fans to the game. "I've always been interested in that period, and when I found out about this game, I immediately wanted to try it," explains Hiroki Tanaka, a nineteen-year-old college student who has translated his love for the period into a new way to part with his money. Forget "Insert Coin"—game screens for games like *Sangokushi Taisen* tell players to "Insert More Coins." One play costs three hundred yen and a starter pack costs five hundred yen. "Card games are extremely popular in arcades," says Nishiyama. "But they're expensive to play, so players expect a high-quality game." Judging

劉備

三国志大戦3軍

桃園の誓い FREE PLAY 再起興軍

SANGOKUSHI TAISEN SCREENSHOT

by the lines of customers, players seem to feel they are getting their money's worth.

"I almost never buy any cards—I usually trade with my friends, but I do spend at least three thousand yen each time I play," says Masayuki Matsushita, a twenty-three-year-old office worker who was introduced to the game by his friends. Matsushita limits his game sessions to the weekend. "I'll come and play on a Saturday or a Sunday, or both days, and will usually end up staying half the day." How much does he spend? "On days when I really get into it, I'll usually spend close to six thousand yen."

Fifty-two-year-old Hiroshi Hamada first played *Sangokushi Taisen* after his college-student son, Masatsugu, got him hooked. "He was the one who started playing these games, and after he told me about them and how interesting they were, I started playing myself." Both father and son love the rich historical tapestry that forms a backdrop to the series, and it's provided a way for them to spend a lot time together. But the game has proven so popular with dad that he now finds himself coming to play by himself. ⟫⟫⟫⟫⟫⟫⟫⟫⟫

"I usually end up playing three or four times a week, sometimes after I'm done work, without my son," explains Hamada.

Here's how it's played: a collection of cards is placed on the playing field (the flat surface of the machine that serves as the card-reading panel). Each card represents a general who is affiliated with one of the game's various factions. There are six factions in the game: the three that represent the main kingdoms of the Wei, Shu, and Wu, as well as a few minor ones that combine various splinter groups. The goal? Lay siege to the enemy's fort with your army of generals. Victory is attained if you manage to bring that fort's "health" meter down to zero, or by maintaining a higher "health" meter total than the fort if the time runs out. As you play the game, you try to position your generals so that they can "smash" their way through the opposition, reducing the enemy general's life total to zero, causing him to retreat, tail tucked between legs. Your own generals can also suffer defeat, referred to with the euphemism "evacuation," when they themselves are forced to, well, evacuate. Generals

LAYING SIEGE TO THE ENEMY'S FORT

in the game are never completely "dead," since those tough-as-nails warmongers return to the battle after a set time. Subsequent versions of the game have offered updates with new characters and factions joining the fray. You can even buy items that can be used in the game from in-game merchants hocking wares. A bit out of the league of illiterate preschoolers like little Ren.

"I like playing the game, and the manga here are free, so I often read a few chapters when I'm here," says Takuya Kasai, a twenty-three-year-old university student, found relaxing between play sessions at the small library of manga on the card-game floor

HOW TO READ YOUR SANGOKUSHI TAISEN CARD

FACTION

BACKGROUND COLOR INDICATES RARITY
In this case, silver means rare card

NUMBER OF ORBS
You can only go to
battle with eight orbs'
worth of generals.

CHARACTER DESCRIPTION
In this case, the
embodiment
of martial arts

CHARACTER'S NAME
In this case, Lu Bu

SPECIAL SKILL
In this case, courage

UNIT TYPE
In this case, cavalry.
Others include spearmen,
archers, sappers,
infantrymen, and
elephant tamers

CHARACTER'S SKILL
In this case,
incomparable strength

STRENGTH
Determines the attack
strength of the unit.

INTELLIGENCE
Determines the unit's
susceptibility to enemy
skills, and also the
strength and length
of the general's skill

**AMOUNT OF MORALE
NEEDED TO USE SKILL**

**RANGE OF
THE CARD**

SANGOKUSHI TAISEN CARDS BY HIRO MASHIMA (LEFT) AND MASATOSHI KAWAHARA (RIGHT)

POPULAR MANGA ARTISTS HAVE CONTRIBUTED ART TO THE CARDS

>>>>>>> of Ikebukuro's Sega Gigo game center. "The storyline of the arcade game is not exactly the same as the ones in the manga versions, but a lot of the characters in the game are taken from them." A few manga series, like Mitsuteru Yokoyama's *Sangokushi* and Hiroshi Motomiya's *Tenchi wo Kurau* (also known as *Destiny of an Emperor* and also adapted into a console series), were inspired by Luo Guanzhong's classic of Chinese literature, *Romance of the Three Kingdoms*. *Sangokushi Taisen* has gone one step further by providing cards that are based on characters from both *Sangokushi* and *Tenchi wo Kurau*. Plus, there are also characters from Yoshito Yamahara's *Ryuroden* (known as *Legend of the Dragon's Son* in English), the story of two junior high school students who find themselves swallowed by a dragon and magically transported to the era of the Three Kingdoms.

Popular manga artists have also contributed art to the cards, such as Hiro Mashima, author of the *Rave Master* manga series,

Jin Kobayashi (*School Rumble*), and Masatoshi Kawahara, creator of the historical martial-arts manga series *Shura no Toki*, and its sequel, *Shura no Mon*. Sitting at the game cabinet, two office ladies in their early twenties—who go by their game monikers Caanan and Agnes—got into *Sangokushi Taisen* because of the pretty cards. "I like the Three Kingdoms Era as a setting, but also was really attracted to the game because of the art on the cards," says Caanan. "A lot of my girlfriends also play for the same reason." (Though Caanan doesn't say whether her friends also have a penchant for calling themselves by their in-game names.) Manga artists from the collective CLAMP have also illustrated a number of cards for ⟩⟩⟩⟩⟩⟩⟩

MOBILE SUIT GUNDAM 0083 CARD BUILDER

AS YOU ENTER the card-game floor of a game center, you can't help but notice *Mobile Suit Gundam 0083 Card Builder* (the 2006 follow-up to 2005's *Mobile Suit Gundam 0079 Card Builder*). Not just because it licenses one of the most beloved Japanese sci-fi franchises, but rather because of the sheer amount of space the game takes up. Inspired by the layout used in *World Club Champion Football*, "pilots" sit in two rows of four, facing a giant screen that is flanked on both sides by two massive robot heads. The screen runs continuous updates of battles currently underway. In the game, you join up with either the Earth Federation Forces or the Duchy of Zeon, with your cards representing the various mechanized units that you bring into battle. As with other panel-equipped arcade card games, you move the cards around in order to battle your opponent, who could be the computer, a nearby player, or someone playing pretty much anywhere in Japan, thanks to the game's network features.

the game. An all-female collective of manga creators, they first exploded onto the scene in 1989 with twelve members and a steady stream of popular self-published works that quickly vaulted them to stardom. Their particular style, one that mixes elements of both boys' and girls' comics, has helped them gain a worldwide following, and they remain a force to be reckoned with, still selling millions of manga despite now having only four members. "Attractive card design is essential," says Yasuhiro Nishiyama. "But the game still has to be fun to play."

Sangokushi Taisen is not the only popular game tempting punters to part with their money. Sega's *Quest of D* series (2004) comes off as a souped-up version of the fantasy hack-and-slash of

QUEST OF D SCREENSHOT AND CARD

old, like Atari's classic 1985 game *Gauntlet*, but with cards. The franchise manages to entice players into its sword-and-sandals world with powerful and appealing characters, and cards, cards, cards. Avatars can be equipped with cards that represent various spells and skills, and as with *Sangokushi Taisen*, a separate smart card is used to save all your game data. The play is more traditional in the sense that it uses a joystick to move your hero around the dungeon, but the game is enhanced by a touchscreen display, where you point to enemies in order to target them, and also to your available spells or skills, which appear on the screen

QUEST OF D MIXES TRADITIONAL JOYSTICK PLAY WITH TOUCHSCREEN CARD PLAY

after having been loaded from the cards that you inserted in the cabinet's reader. Mixing traditional joystick play with touchscreen card play, think of *Quest of D* as being a key link in the arcade-game evolutionary scale.

But it's not all about dudes with swords, but also dudes with balls! Sega's *World Club Champion Football*, aimed at the young-adult and adult market, started the card-based gaming craze in Japan's arcades. Produced in association with collectible sports card maker Panini, *World Club Champion Football* brilliantly combines arcade gaming with collecting sports cards. The soccer game, introduced in July of 2002—the year that Japan cohosted the soccer World Cup and when interest in the sport in Japan was at an unprecedented high—marked the company's first entry into the card-based game genre, and since then the game has been updated annually, adding a growing number of players, teams, and leagues. The first two editions, 2001–2002 and 2002–2003, only covered the Italian Serie A league, but later editions added more European and South American clubs to the mix. Each card represents a real player, culled from the world of soccer. Cards are placed in the card-reading play area, in positions that reflect true soccer positions, and >>>>>>>

WORLD CLUB CHAMPION FOOTBALL SCREEN AND GAME CABINETS

affect the simulated games that follow. The smart card in this game represents your club and you as a manager, and it's where your team's records are saved. As with other card games, the cabinet rewards players with new cards after games, win or lose. The success of the series—the first few years after release saw constant crowds of players and onlookers alike—was in providing an outlet for many a boy's fantasy: allowing them to control their sporting heroes, in a game that saw them take on the role of a team manager. "I first found out about the game on the Internet, and couldn't believe that something like this existed," says Toshihiro Watanabe, a twelve-year-old player who's actually wearing a soccer uniform, as if he just walked off a real-world playing field. "I don't play any other games, only this one because it's about soccer, and I love soccer." Got that?

RARE RONALDINHO CARD

World Club Champion Football has gotten a release in Europe, where soccer—or football—reigns supreme. Although there has been no official

THE iDOLM@STER

THE iDOLM@STER SCREENS (ABOVE), CARDS (BELOW RIGHT), AND GAME CABINETS (BELOW)

If combat and sports aren't your thing, then how about managing your very own pop idol? That's what you get to do in *THE iDOLM@STER*, taking on the role of producer for an idol of your choosing, guiding her career by playing through a series of minigames. The card used in the game represents that idol—you get a different card for each idol whose career you manage—updated with current game data after each play session, and the game is played via the cabinet's touch-screen interface.

The series has found success outside of game centers as a cult hit on the Xbox 360. If the cutesy look of the game and its characters makes you think that this is a game aimed at girls, think again. The game is played by hard-core otaku, who find great satisfaction in seeing their favorite idol strut her stuff in all her cel-shaded glory.

REN WINS A RED KING CARD

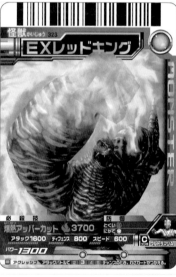

THESE GAMES ARE FOUND PRETTY MUCH ANYWHERE CHILDREN CAN PESTER THEIR PARENTS FOR MONEY

North American release, the city of Miami has seen a few test cabinets. But card games are spreading. *Sangokushi Taisen* has hit arcades in Hong Kong, Taiwan, and Singapore. Games that have made their way out of Asia to North American shores are some of the kids' franchises that many a parent will immediately recognize, like the beetle-based combats of *Mushiking* or the dress-up-and-dance fashions of *Love and Berry*. These games aren't only found in game centers, but in supermarkets, toy stores, and pretty much anywhere children can pester their parents for money. For a generation of kids, these are the types of games they associate with game centers and they regard arcade cabinets that don't spit out cards with suspicion. What's the point of button pressing if you're only going to get a high score? Can't take that home or trade it with your buddies.

Back in front of the Data Carddass *Daikaijyu Battle* cabinet, little Ren shoves a hundred-yen coin in the machine. It spits a card into a vending-machine-style drop slot. He sticks in his hand, yanks it

Daikaijyu Battle cabinet, little

out, and flips it over, glancing at it for less than a second. "It's a double!" he says. His mother checks the card that shows *Ultraman* monster foe Red King and rifles through his *Daikaijyu* card album, finding a page full of Red Kings. It's not a double, little Ren actually already has four of them. He asks his mother for another coin, which he sticks in the cabinet, and they both lean slightly forward as he puts his hand in the slot and pulls out another card. And another. And another. ✱

CARDS, DANCING, AND COMICS

Little girls now have something to tide them over between play sessions of the card-and-rhythm-game hybrid *Magical Dance on Dream Stage*, launched by Disney and Sega in 2007. In April 2008, manga creator Nao Kodaka's *Disney's Magical Dance!!*, a new series based on the game, debuted in Kodansha's *Nakayoshi*, a monthly comic magazine aimed at young girls. This is far from the first property aimed at children to combine gaming and comics in the hopes of bridging the gap between fans of each medium, but it certainly goes to prove that pretty much anything can be turned into a narrative.

MAGICAL DANCE ON DREAM STAGE THE MANGA

INDEX

PICTURE CREDITS

THANKS

Shoko, Renny and new baby for patience, love and soul. Really, for more than words can express.

My parents for everything.

Cathy Layne for being an ace editor, having no preconceptions and becoming a game nerd.

Jean Snow for asking if I had any book ideas, a couple of fantastic interviews and always being up for drinking in the park.

Andrew Lee for totally getting it from the get-go, and layout wizardry.

Yuki Nakano for hanging out in arcade after arcade and taking great picture after great picture.

Yuko Fujiwara for dazzling the bigwigs.

Mr and Mrs Snow for their support, love and having Jean.

Koji Ueda, Taku Sasahara and Shinobu Shindo for trust, belief and access.

Asako Ueno for going the extra mile. Yoshihito Koyama for the fighters.

Shigeru Matsumura for inviting us in.

Minoru Ikeda for the arcade love, the insanity and the unbelievable generosity. Naoya Muramatsu for access. Brian Crecente, Michael McWhertor, Luke Plunkett, Jason Chen and everyone at Gawker Media for their invaluable input. Chris Baker for a career. Ben Judd for never being too leet. Jason DeGroot for 8-bit. Tim Rogers for making stuff happen. Dewi Tanner for class. Ryan Payton for support against the odds. John Drake for rock 'n' roll. Matt Alt for advice. Brendan Koerner for countless book chats. Alice Taylor for encouragement. Chris Kohler for support. Jerry Martinez, Polly Gilbert, Deborah Goodwin, David Patton, Diana Martinez, Andres Chavez and 205 College Ave. for a strong foundation. The Ueda Family for being wonderful. Mikado, Club Sega in Akihabara, Purikura no Mecca, Shibuya Monaco and Taito Hey! for locations. Café Pause for the coffee, the WiFi. Japan Rail for the bullet train. Meat Bun for making delicious shirts.

And of course, all the game creators, companies and players for the insights. Without them there wouldn't be this book—or arcades, for that matter.

BRIAN ASHCRAFT
OSAKA 2008

GAME OVER!
CONTINUE?

（英文版）ゲーセン・マニア
Arcade Mania

2008 年 9 月 24 日　第 1 刷発行

著　者　　ブライアン・アッシュクラフト

発行者　　富田 充

発行所　　講談社インターナショナル株式会社

　　　　　〒 112-8652 東京都文京区音羽 1-17-14
　　　　　電話　03-3944-6493（編集部）
　　　　　　　　03-3944-6492（営業部・業務部）
　　　　　ホームページ　www.kodansha-intl.com

印刷・製本所　大日本印刷株式会社

落丁本・乱丁本は購入書店名を明記のうえ、講談社インターナショナル
業務部宛にお送りください。送料小社負担にてお取替えいたします。な
お、この本についてのお問い合わせは、編集部宛にお願いいたします。
本書の無断複写（コピー）は著作権法の例外を除き、禁じられています。

定価はカバーに表示してあります。

© ブライアン・アッシュクラフト 2008
Printed in Japan
ISBN 978-4-7700-3078-8